WHAT'S RIGHT for all AMERICANS

By Ezola Foster with Sarah Coleman

WRS
PUBLISHING

A Division of WRS Group, Inc.
Waco, Texas

First published in the United States of America in 1995 by WRS Publishing, A division of WRS Group, Inc., 701 N. New Road, Waco, Texas 76710
Book design by Yvonne Chiu
Jacket design by Joe James

10 9 8 7 6 5 4 3 2 1

Library of Congress Catalog Card Number

Foster, Ezola. 1938-
    What's right for all Americans / by Ezola Foster with Sarah Coleman.
    ISBN No. 1-56796-058-8
    1. Afro-Americans--Social conditions. 2. United States--Ethnic relations.
I. Coleman, Sarah Jepson. II. Title.
E185.86.F67   1995
305.8 ' 00973--dc20

                                                                94-48183
                                                                CIP

DEDICATION

When asked if there is an area in which I consider myself a "liberal," I reply that I stand on an extremely liberal platform when it comes to expressing a deep love and appreciation for my husband, Chuck, and our son, Troy. These two strong men are a constant, consistent source of encouragement, support, and joy.

This book is dedicated to them.

WHAT'S RIGHT FOR ALL AMERICANS

TABLE OF CONTENTS

FROM THE COLLABORATOR

I first met Ezola Foster by invitation of Dr. W.R. Spence, the founder of WRS Publishing. He asked if I would meet with her and consider becoming her "hired pen."

I was convinced at first that she had been born somewhere in the affluent South with a "silver spoon in her mouth." I soon learned the opposite, with her message that "poor is no excuse." Her beauty and intelligence are awesome. It was obvious that her values were formed not by the evening news, but by life's experience. She was not the "resident heretic" the liberals loved to attack.

Her life is a portrait of dignity, strength, and character. She has stage presence and a story catalogue that are both inspiring and frightening. Her audience rapport is unequaled. When she speaks, it is like lightning piercing the cloud of discouragement hanging over our inner cities. She is spontaneous and humorous, and her documented findings are as startling as if she had leapt from a plane without a parachute.

I suspect her mother had wisdom in giving her the name Ezola. After months of working, doing lunch, visiting, laughing, and crying together, and of reliving her incredible life, I look at "Ezola" as an acronym:

E   Energy, education, and excellence

Z   Zeal for the cause of restoring hope to the inner city

O   Opinions based on truth and research—and, oh, it is almost impossible to keep up with her!

L   Love for and loyalty to her people

A   America! Restoring its principles and heritage

Sarah Coleman
Wildomar, California

FOREWORD

Who speaks for black Americans? If you buy the conventional wisdom given to us by the network news and the major papers, you might name Jesse Jackson, Maxine Waters, Al Sharpton—maybe even Louis Farrakhan or Ice-T. Ezola Foster shows us, however, that we would do well to reconsider who speaks for blacks.

When Ezola Foster was growing up in the Jim-Crow South, black people confronted naked legal and extra-legal discrimination every day. "Whites only" drinking fountains, "Negroes' Day" at the cinema, and the specter of lynchings were some of the injustices that today's young blacks can scarcely imagine. These injustices were imposed from the outside. Within the black community it was different. Families stayed together. Most children were raised by a mother *and* a father. Crime, drugs, and other forms of social pathology were not a way of life. No one would have thought of glamorizing, in song or fashion, the life of the street gangs and hustlers.

During this earlier period, black men and women of courage and character rose up from our communities to lead our people in protest—peaceful, dignified protest—against the injustices of discrimination. Ezola Foster was there. Like so many others, she was there when civil rights was a righteous cause and morally unambiguous.

Surveying the social and economic landscape of America today, however, one cannot help wondering whether there has been a betrayal of all those who gave their blood, sweat, and tears to end legalized discrimination. While legal racism is gone, the American dream seems even more elusive for many blacks today than it did a generation ago. Not only that, black people rob, murder, and drug one another at unprecedented rates. It is no exaggeration to say that what has become standard fare in most communities never could have happened earlier, even when racism was at its worst.

What happened? Ezola Foster shines her lamp on a tragic truth: somewhere along the way, the civil rights movement was hijacked by a band of "snake oil" salesmen (as she calls these politicians and preachers) who have distorted the dream of a society in which people will be judged "not by the color of their skin but by the content of their character." Civil rights organizations now march to the tune of hustlers and charlatans and receive their sustenance from guilt-ridden white liberals and mau-maued corporate and foundation CEOs. Their job today is to create resentment, division, and dependence.

In some ways, we have reinstilled corrupt practices of the past with simply a change in color. An example of this pattern is the trial and acquittal of Henry Watson and Damien Williams for the merciless beating of Reginald Denny during the Los Angeles riot of 1992. Their act of savagery was captured by television cameras, yet a jury found them innocent of most of the serious charges brought against them. Reverse the colors in this case, and you are back in the Old South, where a white jury would almost never convict a white man of the rape or murder of a black.

All Americans—black and white—need to read Ezola's message. Revenge, reparations, and racial quotas will not solve the problems of the black community. Black people can be their own worst enemies, or they can be their own best friends. We have listened to the snake oil politicians and preachers for too long. Now it's Ezola's turn. She has a worthy message.

—Walter E. Williams, Ph.D.
George Mason University
Fairfax, Virginia

INTRODUCTION

Writing this book has been a real journey into the past. I have relived the days of segregation, the civil rights movement, and the drift toward the socialist ideas that characterize much of the civil rights establishment today.

My concern and love for America led me to form Black Americans for Family Values, now known simply as Americans for Family Values. We are a research and education organization involved in the debate on public policy.

We have been called a civil rights organization, a fringe group, right-wing fanatics, and other names that a lady would not repeat. If conservative means love of God, country, and family, it is a label I wear with pride as I offer in this book my assessment of the problems black Americans face.

As a thirty-year veteran of the public schools, I can say with some authority that taking God out of the classroom has deprived our children of a system of beliefs and stripped them of any principles by which to direct their young lives. The unhappy results of three decades of trying to teach in a moral vacuum are all too plain in the measurements of our children's academic achievement and in their behavior at school and in the street. It is my hope that we will reach a consensus on the need to return sound moral principles to the public school curriculum.

Do our children respect their country anymore? How can they care about America when they are taught to pledge allegiance to Africa or some other foreign land? Hyphenated Americanism is divisive and harmful. The children in every public school in this land should begin each day by pledging allegiance to the flag of the United States of America and to the Republic for which it stands.

The family is too important to be redefined at each presidential election. Promoting family values does not mean

building day-care centers and passing family-leave laws.
Family values demand love and marriage before baby and
carriage. All families, especially those who, for whatever
reason, are headed by a single parent, would only benefit
from public policies based on morality.

I take an unshakable stand on the issues of:

Morality: We are told we cannot legislate morality,
              but immorality is being legislated all the
              time.

Poverty: Being poor means your pockets are
              empty, not your mind.

Education: Children learn best from example; the
              trouble is, they don't know a good
              example from a bad one.

Welfare: Is welfare compassion or another form of
              exploitation? The answer is to be found
              by recognizing who has "fared well." No
              apologies here. I am what you read!

CHAPTER 1
Dangerous to the Cause

Truth is a lonely trail.

I am well acquainted with the isolation of being a voice crying in the wilderness to the majority of today's black leadership, "Let our people go!" Release them from slave masters whose shackles are no less debilitating than those that bound our ancestors on slave ships.

Our people have been tricked, taken, and cheated. Is there no promised land? Radio and television commentators, talk-show hosts, journalists, the clergy, politicians, and the self-appointed spokespeople for blacks are generating much more heat than light. There is no way our problems can be solved by looking to the government alone.

Milton Friedman said it well: "Nothing is so permanent as a temporary government program." Conservatives herald the message "A government that is big enough to give you all you want is big enough to take it all away." Abraham Lincoln, who with an all-white Congress freed the slaves, obviously portended the future:

- *You cannot bring about prosperity by discouraging thrift.*
- *You cannot strengthen the weak by weakening the strong.*
- *You cannot help the wage earner by pulling down the wage payer.*
- *You cannot further the brotherhood of man by encouraging class hatred.*
- *You cannot help the poor by destroying the rich.*
- *You cannot keep out of trouble by spending more than you earn.*
- *You cannot build character and courage by taking away a man's initiative and independence.*
- *You cannot help men permanently by doing for them what they could and should do for themselves.*

We are constantly told, in politically correct rhetoric, that we cannot legislate morality. Yet legislation for immorality proliferates.

I am black and I am an American. Not a hyphenated black-American—an American. I am not ready to pledge allegiance to Africa, as so many of our children are being taught. We are one nation, under God.

I tremble to think of our young children and the curriculum that occupies their minds. I constantly ask myself how will we protect students from the damaged goods they are being sold and the negative thinking that is the rule of their day. I am a proponent of traditional education, where reading, writing, and arithmetic replace racism and revisionist history.

Having been an educator for thirty years, I know that a good teacher explains, a superior teacher demonstrates, and a great teacher inspires. Inspiration does not come with a militant fist.

These are not just opinions, these are my personal convictions. Therefore I am "dangerous to the cause"—the cause of the majority of the black leadership. Why? Because I believe in strong family circles and traditional values. I believe in the right to work and pro-life legislation. Free and fair market capitalism works.

Religious faith permeated the hearts of my people as I grew up in the South. Religious liberty and belief in God led us to worship and helped us move ahead. My church believed that society does not survive without Christianity. A healthy, working religious faith bound us together in spite of the racial intolerance and restrictions of the day.

Moving into college and studying history, I learned that conservative founders like John Adams believed that "the constitution was made only for a religious and moral people." He was convinced that our constitution was totally inadequate for a society of any other kind. America was born to be a nation with the soul of a church. Our hope came from the truth of the Bible—absolutes, not recommendations!

We loved America. We were proud of our flag and of our relatives who served in the armed forces. We lined parade routes and observed our fathers, brothers, uncles, and grandfathers take off their hats in respect when Old Glory passed by. We waved our little flags and sang, "His truth goes marching on . . . and on . . . and on." And so did we.

I believe that the anti-poverty programs of yesterday have become the ill-managed give-away programs of today. A welfare system destroys dignity and does little to provide love and care and hope. Welfare is false compassion. Illegal immigration is just that—illegal. So why have our borders caved in to the politicians? Why does crime continue to escalate after billions of dollars have been lavished on America's inner cities?

I am dangerous to the cause because I move against the current and seek to turn the tide. I want the hidden agendas of the liberals to be revealed, the fear that cripples our communities to be erased, and the majority to again be heard. I am dangerous to the cause because my mission and that of Americans for Family Values is to alert and educate the public.

Yes, I am dangerous to the cause because I speak with authority. Early on I learned that being poor is no excuse. Poverty affects the pocketbook, not the brain. My background was similar to that of the young children who are being used to promote "the cause." My circumstances were those of someone who today is called "at risk": I was poor and from a single-parent home. Now these circumstances catapult certain groups to the forefront in obtaining money and promoting agendas. I was taught the work ethic, that a family should stick together, that picking cotton for college was not demeaning, and that the harder I worked the "luckier" I would get.

For seventeen years I was a Democrat. For seventeen years I have been a Republican—a Republican in the true sense, as in our Pledge of Allegiance . . . "the *Republic* for which it stands." I am convinced that "liberty and justice for all" is not a by-product of a liberal Congress, the liberal press, or opinion-spinners, but the truest meaning of the constitution, which was written by men of character, principle, and faith—men who trusted that those who succeeded them would follow their intent and example.

I believe there is a door to hope for all Americans, no matter their color, creed, or race. If the door appears hopelessly sealed, I seek to take it off its hinges to provide an unimpeded entry, not labeled "Colored only" or "White only," as in my childhood, but an entry to everything that is right and responsible for America and all her people.

THE VOICE OF EXPERIENCE

Often I see parents drop their heads in frustration and hear them say, "If only I could give more and better things to my child." It alarms me because I see many overly concerned about giving their offspring the material things they may have lacked, but in so doing, forget to give them the meaningful blessings they may possess.

I was born in a little postage-stamp-size town called Maurice, Louisiana. The town is a story in itself. My grandparents, Doris and Anastasia Catalon, practically owned the Negro part of Maurice. Their parents, newly-freed slaves, had received their "forty acres and a mule," and my grandfather, innately wise and plantation-smart, made this pay dividends for his family and neighbors.

He knew about slavery, and he had experienced freedom. For him, as for so many in his day, learning and knowledge came from many informal sources. He formed the Society of St. Joseph, an innovative self-help financial organization that was open to the Negroes of Maurice. He was a self-styled entrepreneur, aware that "a good name is rather to be chosen than riches." He shared his modest wealth. Grandfather motivated the people to build a town hall, where the society held its meetings. One of the society's functions was to protect its members and their neighbors from those who had refused to accept the end of slavery. They met with determination and purpose. Hard work, it was taught, would pave the road to success.

He built a Catholic church on his land so that Negroes could worship with the dignity and respect that he believed their Lord and God intended. It was a day of great excitement and affirmation when blacks were afforded the choice of whether to sit in the front or the back of *their* church. Choices were always celebrated. It was quite a contrast to receiving Communion last, at the end of a very long line.

I feel a twinge of nostalgia when returning to the little town of my birth and visiting the church that still stands as a monument to faith and to Grandfather's *freed*-enterprise system. Yet conversely, I mourn, quite disheartened, that a century after his efforts, the town still worships separately.

When I was two years old our family moved to Houston, Texas. My father was in the military and rarely home. Three years later my parents quietly divorced. Mother became a single parent with five children, each two years apart. The youngest, I was always taught to love both parents very much. Mother came from a family of thirteen brothers and sisters. Everyone helped each other. Neighbors looked out for the neighborhood. There was no welfare, no food stamps—just reaching into the reservoir of one's self and drawing out every possible ounce of energy to succeed.

We were disciplined, usually gently, by family, neighbors, and teachers. The psychologists would be stunned to know that I was once whipped with the cord of my mother's electric iron. Thwarted? Not to my knowledge, and I never disobeyed in that way again. I learned fast who wielded authority. That incident never made me want to go out and rob a bank, mug a little old lady, or grow up hating white people because my parents were black. That was not our American Dream.

Of Mother's five children, the oldest was a girl, with three brothers between her and me. We grew up in a low-income area of Houston called Studewood. We all had chores, but it was the task of my brothers to look out for me. My sister was assigned house duty and much of the cooking while Mother worked.

My brothers' ingenuity placed me in an after-school "day care" of their choosing. It was the local Catholic church.

They would take me inside, plop me down on a pew, and tell me to stay there until they returned. They then disappeared to play sandlot ball on the church grounds. Sometimes the priests would join them. But I learned to sit. I would look up at the Blessed Virgin Mary, study the crucifixes and statues, watch St. Joseph, and focus on the stations of the cross. Sometimes I thought the statues were moving. Sometimes I dreamed. Often I fell asleep until they retrieved me from unattended, free ecclesiastical baby-sitting.

In school my three brothers watched out for me. I was never allowed to go any place alone. I could not talk to strangers and was not given the luxury of calling boys on the telephone. A brother was always in attendance except during the countless times I was stashed among the plaster saints at church. The protectionist rule surrounded me through high school. My middle brother married a girl from the Sugar Hill part of the black community. Her mother had worked for "Miss Anne," a rich lady in the affluent section of Houston. She often gave Miss Anne's hand-me-downs to me.

Kids often laughed at me because I talked "funny." I was a Louisianian, and my English was broken up with French Creole. But somehow I garnered respect. I was elected a princess, led more than one class, and was involved in countless activities. Never the best student, I still worked hard.

To my family, the American Dream meant you did not have to grow up with hate to become a celebrity or successful. Success was founded on loving not hating. In this book you will discover that my foundation comes from loving, appreciating, working, and possessing the things necessary for endurance! We often encountered hate, and the way we were taught to handle it was not to hate back. Revenge was never an option. Ours was not an impossible dream that change someday would come. The course was set. It would be possible to fight racism without destroying an entire nation and denigrating an entire people. We learned that truth ultimately prevails. In my early years, I never remember hearing those two now so distasteful words—"black agenda."

We anticipated enjoying life like other Americans: owning a home, having a better car, being able to go to the lake or take a vacation. We looked forward to raising our children and prospering. We did not dwell on how hard we had it or on the problems of our parents and grandparents; we were grateful we had come so far. Advancement may have been slower for some, but there was still progress.

All of my summers were spent with my grandparents in Maurice. We would drive from Houston, and the journey was always an event. Of course, the South was segregated. When we stopped for gas, we could not use the restrooms unless there was one designated for us. To purchase things in the little general stores, we had to enter through the back door. Strangely, it never left a bitter feeling. If there was a rest-stop emergency, we asked the attendant if we could use the bathroom, and we were seldom denied. I don't remember my mother or stepfather ever discussing this "abuse" in our hearing. It was just a part of life, and most of us felt that somehow, some way, someday, those Jim Crow laws would be obsolete.

Those personal experiences make me wonder where the children and activists of today get their hatred and their unbelievable depictions of "our bitter past." In thinking it through, I believe they mostly emanate from the classroom.

In high school I had a history teacher who was militant for that time. She was dogmatic in teaching that Lincoln had little to do with freeing the slaves. She often maintained that he cared nothing about the welfare of the blacks, freeing the slaves only because it was the politic thing to do.

Somehow her words did not ring true. I started reading about our sixteenth president and was impressed by a quite different account. He had opposed slavery before it was the popular thing to do. As a candidate for the senate, he was adamant in wanting to end this injustice. Revisionist history has been with us for a long time.

Today I am appalled that many of our young people are unaware that it was Lincoln who took the stand. They believe freedom for blacks came with the death of Martin Luther King Jr.

The summers in Maurice afforded another surprise. What an occasion it was in the '50s when Negroes were allowed a one-Saturday-a-month movie. My uncle would gather all us children together and march us on the shoulder of Highway 167, which was, and still is, the main street, to the theater. To the excited youngsters, it was like the Yellow Brick Road in *The Wizard of Oz*. Awareness of the discrimination never entered my young mind. It was so exciting to have the theater to ourselves. Relatives sent homemade candy with us to the movie for snacks.

Recreation? We were delighted when there was time for it. We learned to make our own balls out of rolled up newspapers and plastic covers. My first doll was made out of an empty Coke bottle. We cut horsehair, took a stick and put it down the bottle and attached the "hair." That was my treasured "Barbie." The rice fields yielded grain that we would pop for our snack between meals. Sometimes we would sit under a big oak tree and watch the highway, counting the cars and wondering who was driving them. We made up all sort of games to entertain ourselves.

We had white neighbors in Maurice. We ran errands for them. We exchanged eggs, homemade butter, and pleasantries. I remember no demonstrations in Maurice. There were no protests in the street. Our meetings were in homes and our town hall. The people generously pooled their money and energy so no one would go hungry. My grandparents grew potatoes and rice along with their cotton, and seeing to it that all the family and neighbors had plenty was a habitual part of life. Grandfather shared his land with his family, situating them on each side of his property.

Memories of those people—their work and values—are forever etched on my heart. Until the death of my grandmother in 1958, those summers were special. I don't know how my grandfather died, but to his family and neighbors he was a tower, and when the tower fell, the landscape for many black families would never be the same again.

As children we never knew the meaning of the word bored. My mother always had a floor to be swept, windows to be washed, or a yard to be mowed, and we had homework to be completed. We helped at home, we worked hard in school, and sitting down to the family meal around seven o'clock each evening was always a joyful event.

Sometimes on Saturday we would go shopping, where we were allowed. If we got thirsty, we might even snatch a quick drink from a "Whites Only" drinking fountain. Sometimes we got caught and were given a dirty look or told to "watch it." Often, clerks and people on the street appeared quietly to ignore us.

The school day began with prayer and the salute to the flag. It had a calming effect on the children. All these things gave us a sense of importance, a sense of being connected to something and someone bigger than ourselves.

Then there were bus rides. Sometimes the driver let us sit where we wanted. Other times we moved toward the back. It is a gross distortion to say we all were ill-treated. We were not sacrificial lambs.

"Poverty affects the pocketbook, not the brain," we were taught. Grandfather was a great example. My mother learned well. As a single mother for many years, she supported the five of us. She started work in the back of a dress shop. Then one day a woman who spoke French came in. Because Mother knew some Creole, the owner, a Jewish gentleman, had her translate. After that she was brought in as a saleslady. Some disapproved, but the owner was true to his convictions. Mother had quietly broken a racial barrier. It was not in any headlines; there was no march down the street in Houston with banners demanding, "Free the Slaves." She had earned her promotion and she was grateful. We too were proud, for now she made eighteen dollars a week. Eighteen dollars to care for five children! She pulled those ends tightly to make them meet. She worked rain or shine, healthy or sick. I used to dream that someday she would not have to work and I would support her. That day came. For fifteen years I supported her. It was my payback time. She was worthy, an inspiration who never complained.

From family we learned how business works. We were probably unaware that we were being taught by example about the free enterprise system. Sadly, children today have little concept of economics or government. They are ignorant of so much. And most know nothing of another adage: that being poor means you must become more energetic.

Sundays were for church and picnics and visits with members of the extended family. Upon graduation from high school, I received a Delta Sigma Theta Sorority scholarship to enter Texas Southern University (previously known as Texas State College for Negroes). I often say the scholarship got me in, but hard work brought me through. The ancient adage is true, "When you pray, you move your feet." I did, picking cotton in the summer, being the wizard of odd jobs, working in a law office and, in the last years, in the registrar's office at the university.

My youngest brother, Rudy, and I were the only two in our family to graduate from high school. Rudy went into the Navy, then settled in Los Angeles. I graduated from college in May of 1960. It was my plan following graduation to join him in California. Sadly, only a short time before my planned arrival, he died of pneumonia.

I was not deterred from my dream of moving to California. It was not difficult to find a good job, and in 1961 I started work in an office that housed two attorneys and an accountant in South Central Los Angeles. It was an all-black firm, ever enthusiastic not just to succeed, but to excel. One of the attorneys is now a Superior Court judge in California.

Work has always taught me to look for strength in the weak and the best in the bad and to realize that our five senses are incomplete without the sixth sense—the sense of humor! I think, too, of the advice of George Bernard Shaw to a poor but determined actor in London: "Take care to make your lines heard." That I have done ever since I knew what my voice box was for: to be heard—heard for all the right reasons.

VINTAGE EZOLA

The cameras are rolling. One from ABC focuses directly on me, and the local print media have notebooks in hand. The rest of the network reporters are in place. This is another day and another press conference. It is already obvious that the black agenda is in place. Rodney King has been beaten. The preparation resembles the staging for an all-out war. The target is the Los Angeles police chief. Facts are in short supply, anger is high, and, as usual, my point of view is desperately outnumbered.

Like other Americans, I am appalled at the beating of Rodney King, though his record of repeatedly breaking the law and violating parole are public information. However, I am much more appalled that the black leadership are inciting the black community in another attempt merely to add some notches for the cause of "demanded change."

This particular day, Americans for Family Values is showing support for the Los Angeles Police Department and its chief, Daryl Gates. I call him a friend. His door has been open, and he had always shown a willingness to listen. He has made numerous attempts to quiet the storm of impending problems. The majority of his men support him. But he has been labeled an enemy of blacks.

A black cameraman finds his way closer to where I am standing. I have seen him before. He smiles a half-smile and in a muted voice says he is with me and my cause. He wishes he could be more public about his conservative views, but "our" side is not popular. Appearing to film me, he says, "You're like vintage wine, Ezola—you get better with age and the fruit of your lips is truth." Still muffling his words, he continues, "There's more of us out there than you realize. Keep it up. Let's take America back." With those words he returns to his place in the press crew.

Such statements are the lift I need. They are rare, but I know "out there" is a majority of Americans of all races who look at these events as I do. For a moment I feel I am standing alone in some kind of time warp, wondering why so many bow to the myth-makers and to those seeking to distort the past and re-create the future. It is a question with difficult answers, and it haunts me continually. How has it happened that all blacks are portrayed as suffering the same fate as this Rodney King? We do not all advance in the same way, we do not all suffer in the same way, and, God knows, we do not all come from the same places!

Joshua Smith, the founder of the MAXIMA computer business, is nearly a billionaire. He is black and he is rich, but that does not mean that all blacks are to achieve riches. Yet the consensus seems to be that since Rodney King has been beaten, *all* blacks are brutalized by the police. So Chief Gates becomes the fall-guy.

Why do so many black leaders find it to their advantage to look at us collectively when it comes to injustice or suffering, but individually when it comes to our progress and success?

My views on the riots following the first trial verdict have been broadcast, simulcast, and recast. People from all walks of life continue to ask how I could support the Los Angeles Police Department and its chief.

Americans for Family Values has chosen to support the police because we believe that most blacks are law-abiding. Surprised? Don't be. Most people hear only the voices of the very vocal minority. Our people still stop when the flashing lights of a police car signal them to pull over. Blacks are still family-oriented. We are considerate of our neighbors. Many work hard and know where their children are at night. Worship is an integral part of our lives. But the perception of who we are and what we want has been distorted. The truth is, we look at the police for what they are: law-enforcement officers there to keep the peace. One out of four American homes will be the victim of crime this year. In black communities the rate is even higher. Crime and the fear of crime plague most neighborhoods, and our families want a police response when 911 is dialed.

Julian Huxley made a sound statement: "Sooner or later, false thinking brings wrong conduct." Today, these words have become the recipe for riot. False thinking has produced the wrong conduct. Branding the LAPD with the "racist" label does not make it racist in fact, but when this falsehood is repeated enough, people start to believe it.

After riots broke out in Florida in 1989 following the killing of a black motorist by a Latino policeman, Chief Gates had instituted the Community Forum in Los Angeles. This series of meetings between black leaders and the police department was designed as a way to prevent such disturbances from happening in our city. I monitored these meetings from a distance.

In attendance would be prominent blacks representing the National Association for the Advancement of Colored People, the Southern Christian Leadership Conference, and the Urban League, as well as notable members of the black clergy, Louis Farrakhan's Nation of Islam, Mothers of Watts, and the black press, including the widely-published newspaper *Sentinel*. A number of business leaders would also be included.

I have frequently wondered if those in attendance were truly passing on the substance of these discussions to their constituents. Why didn't the most listened-to black radio station make an effort to broadcast the findings and help its listeners know what had been brought up in the meetings? The chief's hope was that this illustrious group would get the word out and teach people how to file complaints and follow up on them when there really was brutality or racism. But the LAPD's message apparently never made it beyond the conference room. Unsubstantiated accounts of racism in the police force, spread by the Black Panthers, raised the volume of the charges and fueled the fires of propaganda. Why didn't the *Sentinel* choose to publish pertinent, impartial views that would inform its readers, quell the storm, and assist the police department? After all, this was the reason the Community Forum was initiated.

Why did these black leaders boycott the Community Forum following the airing of the Rodney King video? Is it possible that they considered it more important to set the stage for control of the Los Angeles Police Department to pass from the people to the politicians by means of a change in the city charter and, ultimately, for the dismissal of Chief Gates?

Compromise was reached in this war for political control of the most powerful domestic "militia" in America—and perhaps the world—in the form of the Christopher Commission, chaired by Warren Christopher, later President Clinton's secretary of state.

The commission was set up to find brutality in the Los Angeles Police Department. It did. The commission was set up to find racism. It did. The commission was set up to get rid of the present police chief and secure a political appointment. It did.

The crescendo of police-bashing continued when the Christopher Commission held hearings to give organizations and individuals a chance to be heard. I will never forget the Friday evening the call came inviting me to represent Americans for Family Values at the hearings. I was scheduled for the following Wednesday at the black-owned South Central Los Angeles Golden State Insurance Company.

At the commission's hearings, we are the only black organization supportive of the police. A true minority with a majority view, we are scoffed at, scowled at, and intimidated. Yet we are undaunted. The cause is too great to be deterred.

The timid cameraman knew. He was not the first to speak of "Vintage Ezola."

As usual, the liberal side is represented with busloads of mostly unsuspecting black families recruited from the Jordan Downs and Imperial Courts housing projects. Their "handlers" know how to get a crowd. The reasons for their participation in a march, a sit-in, or a show-of-force are legion. Some join in for a day away from the confinement of the projects or just for a sandwich and a ride in a bit of the outside world. There are occasional threats of "If you don't all cooperate, those whites will take over!" How I would love to have a definition of "those whites"!

Intimidation and fear mixed with a tangled hope that another day will be better are etched in the faces of those stepping off the rented buses. Those faces tell a story of welfare, false promises, belligerence, and a growing indifference to truth. I cannot help but notice that some of the young children are dressed in the colors of the African National Congress. They are ready for a battle, but their young minds are too inexperienced and unsure to discern what the battle is really about. My heart is heavy as I watch the black masses stream into the auditorium, heavy because I know I am speaking for my people, but they are led to believe that I am the enemy and that I am dangerous to the cause.

Again the media, both national and international, are present. On the carefully crafted agenda, I am the sixth of fourteen speakers. Each of us is sworn in at the beginning of his testimony. Some seem to think that these oaths are all that is needed to legitimate the commission's report.

Somewhat uneasily, my husband and I look around to see if any policemen are among the masses. There are none.

As the proceedings get underway, the first to speak are Father David O'Connel and Humberto Bernabe. They are involved with a few other men and a woman in the Southern California Organizing Committee. Before their testimony, they ask Mr. Christopher to purge the room of all police officers. The reason? They are "afraid of police officers, afraid to speak if police officers are present." The irony of this request is that in 1984 this same group was calling for more policemen in the community. Back then they had said, "Every day criminal warfare is being waged in South Central Los Angeles, and . . . the criminals are winning."

Deferring to their demands, Mr. Christopher clears the room of lawmen. The SCOC representatives then tell of their "abusive" treatment at the hands of the LAPD, much to the delight of that hand-picked audience who loudly roar their approval.

Next on the agenda is the Urban League. The audience stamps and shouts as President John Mack testifies: "If your face happens to be black in this city, you may be an

endangered species if you have to encounter the Los Angeles
Police Department." I keep waiting for specifics,
documentation—there is none—yet the more loudly he
presents his "case," the more loudly the audience cheers
him on.

I seem to remember the former NAACP president,
Benjamin Hooks, giving the real reason that blacks may be
an "endangered species." He said, "The Los Angeles black
community is under siege from drug and gang-related
violence."

My husband, Chuck, and I study the people there—the
speakers, the audience, and the commissioners at the table.
We shake our heads in amazement. This not a hearing so
much as an out-of-control mob. Little is done to bring order.

The third person to speak is the president of the Los
Angeles chapter of the NAACP, Joseph Duff. His testimony:
"There's a perception that the police are racist against blacks
and other disfavored groups. There's a perception that the
police believe that they are above the law . . .," at which
the mob goes wild again and order is hard to restore. The
word "perception" stays in my mind. Again the accusations
were not substantiated, but the crowd does not seem to care.

The tone becomes uglier and more threatening with the
testimony of Michael Zinzun of the Black Panthers. He warns
Mr. Christopher and the rest of the commission that "people
are talking about taking this to the streets, and we ain't
talking about just marching." He continues with the threat of
"another hot summer in L.A.," referring to the Watts riots
some two decades ago. He calls Los Angeles a "powder keg."
By now the noise of the clapping, dancing crowd is deafening.

Next comes Karol Heppe of the Police Misconduct Lawyer
Referral Service. Citing no specific evidence, she says, "We
believe that the Rodney King incident was not an aberration
and have reason to believe through evidence obtained by
our agency and through contacts with other community
agencies that there is a pattern of abuse within the Los
Angeles Police Department." Amid the swirl of the hearings,
I recall that Ms. Heppe's organization worked with "other
community agencies" to bilk the black community out of

more than ten thousand dollars to represent a gangster who had just got out of prison for killing another gangster. They charged that "police brutality" and "racism" were responsible for his troubles.

The crowd's response to Ms. Heppe is more subdued, and I wonder if that's because she is white. I glance around the room again while my husband wisely checks all the exits. We know that I am the next speaker and that Mr. Christopher has dismissed all policemen.

At last, among some mumbling and murmuring, I am sworn in. I know some of the people in attendance. I have taught their children, lived in their neighborhoods; they have seen me on television and read about me in the press. I am sure to disturb the previous speakers since I never mince words and am dangerous to *their* cause.

My words are sure and the audience polite as I express my position. I explain that I believe that the vast majority of the black community is law-abiding, and, while I am appalled at the beating of Rodney King, I urge "that this commission strongly consider the motives of those black leaders who use the name of the black community . . . ."

Before I can finish my statement the crowd has jumped to its feet, stamping, hurling insults, screaming—almost as if led by a conductor. The hooting and howling persist while a bewildered Chairman Christopher sits helpless.

There is very little effort to establish order. When the clamor finally subsides to a low roar, Mr. Christopher suggests that "Mrs. Foster might appear before the commission in private and give her testimony." The audience appears placated. I cannot resist continuing. I say to the chairman, "I was invited here. . . . I would say, Commissioner, that maybe the audience should be removed and I should speak."

The audience disagrees. The insults resume, the obscenities escalate, and there are threats of violence against me and my family. Looking the nine commissioners directly in the eyes, pointing to the mob, I ask, "These are people who say they believe in democracy, and they will not let me speak?"

By now books, notepads, and pens are flying at me.
Suddenly I realize that I am at the mercy of a hostile crowd
with no protection other than my husband. The Christopher
Commission is immobile. I know it is time for us to "git outta
Dodge." Gleaming television lights are focused on the exit,
but they don't deter the insults and threats that followed us
out the door or the people who trailed us into the parking lot.

It was with relief, mixed with pain, that we drove away
from the debacle. I was never again called to appear and
give testimony, not even in private. My prepared testimony
for the committee was fully documented.

What were they afraid of? Why had the commission
denied a private citizen the right to speak? Was I a danger
to the cause? Then *whose* cause? Did the commission want
full representation? Obviously not!

Discouraged? Yes, but not enough to stop spreading the
message that one day change will come in spite of the
impediments. Poverty is not the only breeding ground for
crime. This escalating war of bigotry and paranoia serves
no one. Human hearts have to change. I am reminded of
these lines from G.K. Chesterton:

According to most philosophers, God in making the
world, enslaved it. According to Christianity, in making it,
He set it free. God had written not so much a poem, but
rather a play; a play He had planned as perfect, but which
had necessarily been left to human actors and stage
managers, who had since made a great mess of it.

I remain dangerous to the cause because I know for sure
that neither the Republicans nor the Democrats, neither
liberals nor conservatives, neither the strident leadership
nor the vocal minority of any color, race, or creed will bring
change without the missing ingredient of truth. The human
actors and "stage managers" have mostly succeeded in
making things worse. We will remain in a mess until values
are instilled and the highest word is heeded: "The truth
shall make you free"—the truth about ourselves, our
communities, and America.

CHAPTER 2
I Pledge Allegiance
To America or Africa?

I n an elementary school classroom, a group of third-graders were about to present a play. It was a celebration of Betsy Ross, George Washington, and the designing of the American flag. The chairs were in place for ten-year-old Todd (a.k.a. George), nine-year-old Elizabeth (a.k.a. Betsy), and another youngster, Denzill Williams. Denzill was dressed in a three-piece suit that didn't quite fit, but he well represented Robert Morris, the mostly-forgotten man who helped fund the American Revolution.

With amazing maturity the children recounted the story of our early forebears and their desire to build a strong United States of America. On the wall behind the chairs was a calendar with the year 1776. With great aplomb Betsy Ross's modern stand-in sewed together the flag that would fly high over America in the years to follow. Scene One ended with the Pledge of Allegiance.

The youngsters told the story of the "Star-Spangled Banner" in the second scene. The calendar was changed to 1814, the year Francis Scott Key penned his magnificent lines about that flag after witnessing the battle of Fort McHenry in Baltimore Harbor. I have always loved the last stanza, which ends:

> Blessed with vict'ry and peace,
> May the heav'n-rescued land
> Praise the Power that hath made
> And preserved us a nation!
> Then conquer we must
> When our cause it is just,
> And this be our motto:
> "In God is our trust."
> And the Star-Spangled Banner
> In triumph shall wave

O'er the land of the free
And the home of the brave.

Who would have dreamt that two centuries later this
emblem would be under attack from Americans?

In days past, most of our children knew that in 1931 the
"Star-Spangled Banner" was made our national anthem by
an act of Congress. In my schools the flag had a place in
our lesson plan. Most black homes displayed the flag. We
were taught to revere it, to honor those who died for it, and
to wave it proudly on the Fourth of July. To have burned it
would have been perceived as a cardinal sin. Can you
imagine my dismay and heartache when I attended my
father's funeral in Houston in 1990 and saw that the flag
displayed in our Catholic church was the African National
Congress flag? Today, many high schools do not have an
American flag in the classroom. There is no recitation of
the Pledge of Allegiance. In elementary and middle schools
in Watts and South Central Los Angeles, saluting the flag is
not mandatory. There is a growing disdain and total lack of
respect for it in this country. Appalled? The same may be
true in the community in which you live.

A black couple visited New York's Whitney Museum of
American Art. They were dumbfounded to be offered, on
leaving, a button that stated, "I can't imagine ever wanting
to be white." Absurd? Denigrating? Outrageous? Yes. But
they reacted with greater shock some months later when
their son came home from a segregated school with a copy
of a different flag salute. The sheet their son held in his
hand was a salute to the flag of the *African National Congress.*

Later in the same year, this couple read a short article in
Reader's Digest that explained the button they were offered
on leaving the Whitney. The article noted the museum's
statement regarding the button in question: "The catalogue
explained that 'whiteness is a signifier of power' and wearing
the button lets whites 'absolve themselves of some of the
privileges of cultural imperialism.'"

The article went on, "By Whitney Museum standards,
almost any angry sentiment seemed to qualify as art. . . . In
two numbing hours at this organized shambles, I learned

that the world is neatly divided into good and bad. Good: women, nonwhites, homosexuals, transvestites, gang members, people with AIDS. Bad: the United States, straight white males, family, religions and hierarchies."

On a recent television talk show, a young black woman wondered whether America should have more than one flag? She was followed by a black high school student obviously indoctrinated in African allegiance. He talked of "correcting history and . . . all the things Africans (the first people on Earth) invented before any other race existed." He preached the gospel of a different flag.

I see and hear these arguments by our black leadership infiltrating the educational system. The question of which flag to salute (if any) is not uncommon. There are too many young children who do not even know there is a flag to salute.

I have seen the motivation of too many civil rights organizations, and it is clear to me that their cause and mine are diametrically opposed. They defy America and perpetuate friction among the races, and now they are even trying to build a case for reparations. The flag they are flying over our people is a foreign flag to me. My cause is to restore faith in America. We have our problems, but this is still the greatest nation in the world. I truly love America and thank her for the opportunity she gave to me. I hope and pray the freedom I enjoy is not a selective freedom with different standards for different races or cultures. My love for America is the kind of love that is something you do—"Love with its sleeves rolled up!"

HYPHENATED AMERICANS

Defining blacks and their history can be confusing. The dictionary definition of Negro is: "a black person; a member of the dominant group of mankind in Africa, living chiefly south of the Sahara and characterized generally by a dark skin." Negro, by my youthful definition, came to mean someone whose ancestors were slaves. In the 1960s the new black leaders wanted to rename us. We were to be black-

Americans. Then it was Afro-Americans. Then it was African-Americans. At the same time we were lumped into a category called "people of color." These same leaders were upset when we were called "colored people." "People of color" does not sound much different to me, and I have to ask myself, "What's the difference?" There must be a specific reason or two for these multiple changes in the proper and improper ways to refer to us.

After the civil rights movement of the 1960s, it became politically incorrect to refer to us as Negroes. The media even received notices to that effect. The purpose was clear: Americans of color were to be associated with the black movement. It was a regrouping attempt.

Now in the 1990s we are redefined as African-Americans, which is yet another political label. This represents an effort, in my opinion, to align us with the ANC in South Africa, to give that organization a platform in America to use as a power base and to raise funds.

> There can be no fifty-fifty Americanism in this country. There is room here for only one hundred percent Americanism.
>
> Theodore Roosevelt, July 19, 1918

It is an interesting question to pose to our hyphenated young people: are you 50 percent African and 50 percent American? Which half serves you best? To which country on the African continent do you pledge your allegiance? Sometimes they answer that their true identity arose during and after the '60s, when blacks started promoting black power.

I see this attitude today on the playgrounds and in the school yards. Children drilling in uniforms like little soldiers, training with a purpose. The majority of our citizens is unaware of the result. That is what happened in South Africa. The leadership there indoctrinated the children, and they became the future militant leaders. Many youngsters between six and fourteen years of age were placed in PLO training camps and then returned to South Africa. They knew how to fire-bomb the houses of people who did not go along with the ANC. They knew the true meaning of the "necklace"—the kind that Winnie Mandela often said would help free Africa as she stood, fist clinched and an arm rigidly pointed skyward.

Attitudes like these have to be taught. Black people do not wake up one morning, yawn, and say, "Today I am going to start hating America!" They are taught that hate.

I tell people in my audiences that there is no such thing as an African-American. When hyphenation is the rule, the outcome will most likely be allegiance to Africa and hostility to America. It is not surprising. Black leaders insist that white America does not care about kids and cares even less about black kids. They do not tell them about the billions of dollars that have been invested in our communities— federal funds earmarked to educate minority children under the Elementary and Secondary Education Act.

"Black power" teaches children to hate. Hyphenation dilutes allegiance. I say it often with pride and gratitude: I am *one hundred percent* American. For that reason I founded Black-Americans for Family Values. Then one day the implication of this name struck me like lightning. The name was hyphenated. The very thing our organization was against was defining us. In keeping with our belief that hyphenated Americans keep the flames of racism burning in this great nation of ours, we immediately changed our name. We are now Americans for Family Values. This expresses our true belief. We are Americans. Being black is not the issue.

In a speech to the Knights of Columbus in New York in 1915, President Theodore Roosevelt put the matter in perspective, as he often did.

> *There is no room in this country for hyphenated Americanism. . . . The one absolutely certain way of bringing this nation to ruin, of preventing all possibility of its continuing to be a nation at all, would be to permit it to become a tangle of squabbling nationalities.*

James Thurber reminds us that "a pinch of possibility is worth a pound of perhaps!" Not all the reasons people started hyphenating themselves are bad. Perhaps they thought that poor people, those descendants of slaves, would take pride in identifying themselves with a distinctive culture. Nevertheless, I believe that neither blacks nor whites nor any other ethnic group needs a hyphen for identification. The playing field today is more level than it has ever been. We can be different and still be equal. The time has come to drop the hyphen.

Henry Cabot Lodge spoke plainly on this issue:

> *If a man is going to be an American at all, let him be so without any qualifying adjectives; and if he is going to be something else, let him drop the word American from his personal description.*
>
> *Hyphenation must end for the sake of progress and national reconciliation. After all, our nation was founded on the unhyphenated principles of human dignity, human rights, and government by the people. Surely "American" is more than adequate for all of us who share a love for the principles of our nation's founding.*

CHAPTER 3
Double Jeopardy

In southern California, where I live, small tremors are an ordinary part of life. But when a real earthquake hits, you know it. The room vibrates like an off-balance washing machine. Our country has been rocked by two tremendous social earthquakes: first, the shift from independence to dependence, from individual initiative to a dignity-robbing surrender to welfare, and second, the thundering tide of illegal immigration.

Who's to blame? To my mind, the guilty parties are the social engineers who continue to design a bigger and more generous welfare state that is open to all comers, legal or illegal. In the court of Real Life they have been tried and convicted, but in the court of Big Government they're always "not guilty by reason of good intentions." They get one new trial after another, while it's America that's in double jeopardy.

WELFARE DEPENDENCY

My mother certainly met the criteria for welfare. She worked hard and long. She was up before dawn's early light to prepare for another day and to catch the bus that took her to work. Her life was marked by courage and endurance, grace and faith, gratitude and humility. She would accept no excuses for being late or unprepared. Sickness never kept her from duty. She put in a full day and then some. Then she climbed back onto a packed bus, usually standing room only, to come home. Her paycheck had to feed, clothe, and care for herself, her five children, and maybe a neighbor in need. Her struggle was personal. She was the breadwinner, the coach, the doctor, the counselor, the consoler. She disciplined us and played with us and made us proud to be family. She taught us that cleanliness is next to godliness, and she accepted no song and dance if we wanted to miss church. She was a pioneer equal-opportunity employer: each of us had duties to fulfill according to age and ability.

"Perform or perish" was Mother's unspoken rule. We knew she meant business. Doing our work gave us a healthy inward feeling of accomplishment and of being needed.

After several years, Mother met and married a man who became a good stepfather, but she kept up her standards of excellence and the desire to achieve. She was fair to us and to her neighbors. Her word was bond.

In today's political climate, Mother's situation would make her the perfect candidate for the public dole. If she had brought her family to California in the 1990s, she could have lived in one of the housing projects and picked up a regular welfare check. She could have . . . but she never would have. Mother may not have realized that the Bible admonishes man to work more that nine hundred times, but she did know that faith and work go together.

Welfare? The definitions vary, but there is one essential truth about it, which Rush Limbaugh characteristically exposes:

> *To liberals, compassion means expanding the dependency cycle and spreading the misery among that ever-growing dependency class. What's worse, another class of people—those who make a living in the massive welfare bureaucracies—has been empowered by what can only be characterized as institutionalized oppression. Ever wonder why no welfare bureaucracy has ever solved a problem and been disbanded? Because those who work in them depend on them for their livelihood. They literally have a vested interest in ensuring that conditions never really improve. In fact, if conditions deteriorate, the welfare bureaucracy expands. This is yet another reason that the problems of our inner cities have become progressively worse, even though the federal government has poured more than $3.5 trillion into social programs since the Great Society programs of the '60s.[2]*

Somehow we can't resist new welfare experiments. The latest one in California—called "work pays"—is supposed to encourage school-age welfare mothers to stick with their education and to encourage older recipients to get jobs. Donna Shalala, the secretary of health and human services, believes it will test ways recipients can achieve self-sufficiency. California's governor, Pete Wilson, wanted to curtail higher benefits for women who had additional children while on welfare, but his program was rejected by the Democrats. The only thing that really changes in the game of welfare reform is the players. Programs proliferate while taxpayers pick up the tab for one failure after another, generation after generation.

In my thirty years in the Los Angeles schools, I have observed that black families resent their welfare dependency. When schools have free food programs, most of the kids dislike them. They throw the food all over the lunchroom. They make fun of the programs. I wish I could capture their feelings, aggression, and waste for the taxpayers to see. What a shock it would be! Some schools have tried to reject free food programs because of the rebelliousness they incite in the very people they were designed to assist.

Welfare dependency hurts families in many ways. For instance, a welfare child's school must certify his attendance every month. This requirement can be a potent weapon in the hands of self-serving administrators to stifle parents' complaints about their children's schools. I have seen schools withhold attendance slips because parents have complained about the quality of their children's education. There was one mother who was alarmed by the immoral sex education in her child's school. When she spoke out, she found her welfare in jeopardy. Her story spread through the projects like wildfire, frightening other parents from speaking out for what was right. When you're on welfare, you learn quickly that biting the hand that feeds you is a bad idea. It is an inescapable reality of welfare programs that, no matter how well intended they are, they subject their beneficiaries to the power of bureaucrats.

On a talk show, I was asked who benefited the most from our government's system of aid. You don't have to be a genius to answer that one: not those who are truly in need, but those who run—and perpetuate—the system. Americans have great hearts when it comes to helping. They rally to give assistance voluntarily when it is needed. But it is no help to enroll people permanently in a miserably failing system.

Rescue missions on skid rows appear to have much more success at rehabilitation than our public welfare system does because they distinguish between those who are totally dependent and those who can be returned to the work force and can regain their dignity.

The Denver Rescue Mission serves many homeless blacks. It tries to bring the needy in from the street, evaluate them, and then send them through either of two doors. Those who are able go through the door that swings wide open to help them become self-sufficient. This door leads back to the world of work and family. The others, who are truly helpless, are given the assistance they need.

Revolutionary? Not at all. That is the way welfare should be—helping people to help themselves and providing for those who can't. Simply building more shelters tends to shelter the homeless from the real world and meaningful self-sufficiency.

I am well acquainted with the welfare system. A friend I grew up with escaped the system as a child but found herself forced to use it as an adult. Dora had come to Los Angeles from Houston a year or so before I did. While she did not have a college education, she was faring quite well. She had a job and her own apartment and was starting to settle into a rather good life. Then Dora, who was not married, became pregnant.

Her boyfriend came from our old Houston neighborhood. Today people would say he was a "stereotypical African-American male," and he acted as many do—he deserted her. Dora lost her job and was alone.

Her alternatives were limited even though she had job skills. In the early '60s, being on welfare was still not socially acceptable, so it was very much "our secret." We talked about it, cried about it and rationalized it, but ultimately had to accept it. Going on welfare was like having the plague to Dora.

Within a year of the birth of her daughter, Dora enrolled in beauty college. She found a job as a beautician and took herself off the welfare rolls. It was an accomplishment we both celebrated. She continued to make progress. She obtained a real estate license and was successful. I will never forget the day we toasted her success in the house she purchased for herself and her daughter.

Dora was on welfare less than two years. It had accomplished its purpose of helping her sustain her family while she learned to rely on herself. Where did she get the gumption to succeed? Perhaps it was her upbringing or just old-fashioned pride. After all, blacks too can be "steel magnolias."

The original purpose of welfare—to help people like Dora back on their feet—has degenerated to planting their feet in cement. California, with its generous welfare system, is a good example. The state has more than its share of unmarried young women who move there because they are pregnant. And unlike Dora, they usually lack the pride and initiative to move on. In a welfare system that makes it easy to get on with no incentive to get off, these girls follow a depressingly predictable path.

Today's welfare system is like the slave trade. On this point, Surgeon General Joycelyn Elders is right (for once): "If you are poor and ignorant with a child, you're a slave." Slaves depended on their masters for their food, shelter, and clothing. Welfare recipients depend on the government for those same necessities.

The incentive for breaking the bonds of slavery was the desire for more than just food, shelter, and clothing. The same desire is necessary to break the bonds of welfare dependency. You've got to desire *freedom*—the freedom of choosing what you eat and where and when you eat it; the freedom of choosing where you live and what you do for a living.

Slaves were hindered in their pursuit of freedom by being denied an education. Today, the public education system, which is dominated by the teachers' unions, combined with the "receive-as-much-as-you-would-earn" welfare system, provides a false sense of freedom and is leading to the re-enslavement of our people.

The pressing need is to find a way out. John Perry Jr. writes, "Figuring out how to get out of this mess we call the welfare system is a lot like trying to get out of quicksand. The more one struggles, the deeper one sinks. The main evil of the welfare system is not the tax dollars, but the human potential it wastes. For far too many welfare recipients, the system suffocates their ambition, incentive, and hope."

Mr. Perry suggests the only way out: "The success of any state welfare agency is how many able-bodied people it can get off the welfare rolls and onto the payrolls. And there should be definite penalties for keeping able-bodied people on welfare year after year."

The story of Star Parker, the founder of the Coalition on Urban Affairs, sums up the problem with welfare. For her, welfare once bore a stigma, but things soon changed.

> The option to receive a welfare check, food stamps, and a Medi-Cal card was an acceptable way of life. The fourth time I found myself pregnant, without a husband, my first thought was to apply for Aid to Families with Dependent Children. By this time, during the early '80s, the welfare system had lost its innocence. Los Angeles County did not require knowing who the father was as a condition of assistance, and on the day my social worker was to visit my home to determine eligibility, she called and told me she was more interested in having lunch with her friends than coming over to check for a male present. Even the hospital didn't require me to identify the father.
>
> Moral attitudes had changed so much since the 1960s that a discussion with the father about how to financially support the newly-forming child never took place. Although we had both passed high school courses

*in sex education, obviously something was being missed
in the curriculum.*

*Regardless of education or socio-economic status,
dependency on government assistance was on the rise
for unmarried, pregnant women.*

Star's story has been repeated a million times over. And
only a few of the characters in this story ever confront the
folly of it, as Star did. When will we see that the welfare
emperor has no clothes?

ILLEGAL IMMIGRATION

It was a magnificent morning in Southern California.
My husband and I were having coffee and discussing the
morning newspaper. The immigration issue was headlined.
The soaring cost and bankrupting effect it has on our border
states are frightening.

Chuck grew up in California from the time he was three
years old. We both have lived in South Central Los Angeles
for most of our lives. So when we speak, it is from experience.
Chuck likens the flood of illegals coming into the United
States to hard-working parents who come home every
evening to prepare dinner and discover there is another
mouth to feed. This happens day after day, year after year,
radically increasing the family size. However, their paychecks
remain the same.

So it is in the taxpaying American family. The ever-
increasing tide of illegals coming across our borders sends
our costs spiraling upward while our resources remain static.
Recent immigrant reform legislation comes nowhere near
to controlling our borders, while amnesty provisions create
a license for wholesale fraud in obtaining precious American
citizenship.

The failure of the federal government to stem this tide of
illegal immigration, coupled with the explosion of illegal
aliens' "rights" that have been established through litigation,
has had a devastating impact on countless black Americans

who are facing the very real possibility of a complete reversal of the civil rights gains made during this century. The legal battles to grant citizens' rights to illegal aliens have fueled a bitter confrontation between Hispanics and blacks as they vie for federal and state social services and welfare programs. The business community must be made aware that cheap labor subsidized by government health and welfare programs is a short-term gain with disastrous long-term consequences.

Having lived and worked in what was once the totally black community of Watts, I have witnessed a striking shift in its ethnic character during the past decade. Watts is no longer a black community; much of it is populated by illegal immigrants. A tour of the public schools in Watts and many other areas of the city will provide convincing evidence of this change.

This influx in Los Angeles, as in other areas of the country, has created an environment where blacks—young and old—are being forced to compete with these illegals in the labor market. Entry-level jobs in fast-food franchises are being filled by illegals who use our public health care support and welfare system to help sustain their dependent families.

The entry-level jobs were once one of the tickets out of the ghetto and into economic independence for enterprising young blacks who were willing to work their way up as far as their ingenuity and hard work could take them.

The signs of doom for black economic upward mobility could not be more visible than on the city's street corners, where "day workers" congregate, waiting for work. Two or three illegals can be hired for the same pay as one black youth, who is told he must be paid minimum wage. Organized labor and the "system" have now priced him out of the job market.

The future for young blacks does not look as bright as it once did. I deeply fear that the civil rights gains which made black Americans proud may be lost because of corporate greed and the failure of the federal government to protect our borders.

In 1986 the Los Angeles City Council took specific steps to create a sanctuary for the undocumented in the city.

Further steps in the 1990s restricted cooperation between the LAPD and the Immigration and Naturalization Service. It was amazing the way the press covered up the immigration problems of Los Angeles. Some called it a great blockade of truth.

The Voice of Citizens Together points out that "this is not a racial issue, it is an economic, ecological and social survival issue." President Glenn Spencer likens the situation to that in France in 1993, when the center-rightists won the biggest parliamentary electoral victory in twentieth-century French history. Spencer notes that the Gaullist Pierre Lellouche even referred to the riots in Los Angeles as proof that immigration can lead to serious problems. Although the American press as a whole reported on the prominence of the immigration issue in the French election, it was mostly ignored by the press in Los Angeles. France has taken immediate measures to halt immigration.

It is obvious that the people of California are frustrated and angry about the government's unwillingness or inability to control the flow of immigration. In November 1994 they passed Proposition 187, the "Save Our State" initiative, which restricted state benefits to legal residents.

California is not the only state in financial straits, but it is home to 52 percent of the nation's illegal alien population. Citizens have a right to demand that their taxes be spent on legal residents. The S.O.S. initiative provides that "illegal aliens will not receive public benefits, paid for by the taxpayers," and requires government agencies to report illegal aliens to the INS.

The severity of the problem is evident from the number of illegal immigrants behind bars. Illegals constitute more than 15 percent of the state prison population in California. Courtroom observers have noted that, at times, illegals make up 50 percent of the criminal case load. The law requires that a defendant be provided with an interpreter at trial if he does not speak English, further increasing trial costs.

Liberals keep saying that America is the melting pot of the world, that America has always been willing to take in those who needed a better life. The words of Emma Lazarus,

"Give me your tired, your poor . . . ," are being turned on their head. At one taxpayers' rally for S.O.S., a husky voice carried throughout the room, "I am the tired and the poor—tired of the problems our government has created and poor from being taxed for those who illegally cross into the United States of America."

The time has come for the politicians to be honest with the people. The costs are horrendous. The S.O.S. initiative is expected to save over $400 million annually on welfare, $1.5 billion on education, $500 million on health care, and $500 million on law enforcement.

Is it cruel and unjust to restrict our borders? Not when serious researchers and writers say that the Los Angeles riot had its roots in massive immigration. In San Diego County, the net cost of illegal aliens exceeds the budget deficits for the county and its cities. In Los Angeles County, 63 percent of the births in public hospitals in 1991 were to illegal aliens. Each year the rate has increased, and each child automatically becomes an American citizen with all of a citizen's rights and privileges. Our common language is being eroded along with the meaning of citizenship. And if all of this does not prove that it is cruel and unjust *not* to restrict our borders, the bottom line remains: illegal is illegal.

In the campaign for S.O.S., I heard many different viewpoints on immigration. A day laborer from El Salvador who came here for work to support his family back home said he deserves a better life. But he failed to answer one question: At whose expense?

An Asian-American noted that she was an ethnic Chinese, born in America. She related that after living in South Central Los Angeles for forty-three years she was swept out by the flood of immigrants, which changed the shape, condition, and environment of her neighborhood. If these people have no respect for the federal immigration laws, she asked, then why would we expect them to obey our other laws once they are here? That's not racism. It is a legitimate concern for our sovereignty.

A priest said that Los Angeles was built by people from different countries. They deserve our support in their time of need. Answering him was a former Mexican who had recently become an American citizen. Quietly she announced that she did not want the state of California to become a Third World country where people are living outside the law. In somewhat broken English she lobbied for English to be the common language.

This whole issue is interesting for me because I am in a school where a number of the students are illegal immigrants or the children of illegal immigrants. Sometimes they come to school all excited and say, "Oh, Miss Foster, I saw you on TV" or "I saw your picture in the paper." When I ask them what they heard me say, they usually comment only on what they saw. "You look so pretty," they say, or they tell me how happy their parents were to recognize me. But often that is where the conversation ends. They are silent on the real issue. If I do engage them in a discussion, there is no problem or resentment. They listen and raise their concerns, but I still tell them, "illegal is illegal." I am up-front with my students about the need to close our borders, our highways, airways, and waterways. Solving this problem will take drastic action.

It is unfair to have a policy that children who cannot speak English can stay in school until they are twenty years old when American citizens who may only be in the eighth or ninth grade at the age of eighteen are kicked out.

In many of our overcrowded schools, some of the older boys often come back in Mondays and tell their friends how they have gone back to Mexico and brought back another load of illegals. They were paid for it. They laugh at how easy it is. We have become a laughingstock. Our government has failed us. I am a firm believer that a country which cannot control its borders cannot protect its citizens. It is that simple.

What do we do? Make our voices heard! Demand that each person running for political office make clear his stand on illegal immigration. Immigration is a hot potato in Congress and in the states. There is new momentum for overhauling the current laws. The opposition to reform continues to come from human rights groups and immigration lawyers. With the billions collected by illegals each year in our nation, change will be slow. America will continue to be more open to immigrants than other nations. The legal and illegal will keep knocking. How the door is opened affects us all.

CHAPTER 4
Who's Minding the Children?

Who is minding our children? Their friends have fallen to urban crime, their families are disintegrating, and, most tragically, they have lost their precious innocence.

WHEN CHAOS IS NORMAL

Violence has become a part of daily life for most inner-city Los Angeles youngsters. Kids take for granted walking into a school through metal detectors. Many classrooms and teachers' rooms are locked. Bars are common decor. The halls and school yards are patrolled by guards. A fourth-grader conceals a knife in his pencil box. Drugs are sold in corners and cubicles and playgrounds.

As I observe this first hand, I wonder whether children are being anesthetized or desensitized to violence. There is a difference. Anesthesia puts someone to sleep. Desensitization allows him to live and function in unpleasant conditions and tolerate them, accepting their horrors. Despite the abundance of studies of the long-term effects of violence on society, particularly children, the violence continues to out-pace the solutions.

And what are the "solutions" that we try? At best, they are just expensive bureaucratic Band-Aids. At worst, they are part of the problem. My blood boils when I step into a government-supported daycare center that operates on the assumption that children two, three, and four years old have rights and interests opposed to their parents, who, according to these bureaucrats, do not always know what is best for their children. We are channeling countless Head

Start dollars into baby-sitting factories where discipline is utterly unknown. How do we expect these kids to turn out?

What a devastating contrast to my childhood. I was physically, emotionally, and spiritually supported. We were able to play outdoors without having to worry about dodging bullets. A loving extended family protected me. No agency ever tested my stress level to see if Mother was raising her family in the politically correct way. She passed on those values instilled in her by her parents and grandparents. You see, most slaves and sharecroppers had integrity. The necessity of hard manual labor never got in the way of doing what was right.

There is no reason these values can't be instilled in children today, even those children whose mothers have to work. Four decades ago, a woman named Charlesetta Childs showed us how to do it. Charlesetta had been a housemaid and "mammy" to a white landowner's children. Freedom gave her the opportunity to follow a long-held dream. With meager funds and lavish hopes, she used her modest dwelling in south Georgia to care for children of working mothers. Her neighbors and others lent a hand. Some of her helpers could not read, but the ones who could taught the others. Charlesetta's wisdom and values are enshrined in the following lines, discovered after her death. They show how she gave her many charges a real "head start" toward a better future long before the "enlightenment" of the 1960s and beyond did its work.

> *Children, you respond*
> *Like flowers to the sunlight.*
> *Being attracted*
> *To the people that*
> *Help you grow.*
> *As teachers*
> *We see ourselves*
> *Reflected in your little lives.*
> *Do you see ourselves*
> *Reflected in your lives?*
> *Children, you respond*
> *To people who love you,*

Who understand you,
And make you feel important.
We love you.
We see you and feel you.
Your hurts are important.
We listen while you help us
Realize how frightening the world is to you.
You view from a different perspective
For you look up . . . to us.
Lord, give us patience
And noise-tolerance
To cope with children long enough
To lead them in the right way
Which is the only way out of confusion.
Help us to consider the children
No less people than ourselves.
And let us help them look even higher
Beyond the teachers . . . to You.

Where have the Charlesettas gone? Why have they been replaced by those who care more for a cause than for children?

THE TEN SUGGESTIONS

Many of our problems in raising children these days go back to the ideas of John Dewey, "the father"—unfortunately—"of American education." Dewey taught that *what* a child learns is not as important as *how* he learns it. In the '60s, activists who saw children as the ticket to regrouping black communities took Dewey's theory and ran with it. They've been running ever since.

Thirty years later we have a curriculum more concerned with how Johnny "feels" about being black than with teaching him history. And if Susie is "comfortable" with two plus two equaling five, why should she be thwarted or discouraged? She has the right to her individual thinking. Self-expression is more important than mere "facts."

This is what I call unconscionable, incompetent baby-sitting in our schools. Scores of "educational" programs are nothing more than platforms for political activists. Education has been replaced by indoctrination.

SAT scores are in a free-fall. The solution? Review the questions. Could it be they were written by a white person? Is this fair to blacks? While the government and educational bureaucrats dither over such questions, the free-fall gathers speed. If our schools only stuck to standards, SAT scores would not be such a problem.

But *whose* standards? my opponents will ask. Whose values? And that, as far as they're concerned, is the end of the discussion. In the 1960s, the courts expelled God from our schools, and when He left He took absolutes with Him. When you make it illegal, as it is in the United States, to post the Ten Commandments in a public school, you do more than expunge formal religion from your children's school day. You create a void where there used to be a system of beliefs about right and wrong. When children are left with the Ten Suggestions (if that), is it any wonder that Johnny can't read and write, but he can graffiti and fight?

The experiment of living without absolutes has had disastrous results. Fortunately they have finally spawned a revolution among black parents, grandparents, and guardians who know their own history and understand that knowledge is the door to opportunity. Ignorance is slavery.

ARE VOUCHERS VALID?

Linda Lofton is the courageous mother of ten children and was a student of mine in Watts. When her eldest son, Robert, was in school at the neighborhood public junior high, he became the object of threats from gang members, who gave him the choice of being a member or a victim of their gang. Robert went to the school authorities but was told that nothing could be done until he was actually attacked. As he told me, "They had to see blood or a dead body before they would help me." Robert left school.

When the Los Angeles public school system threatened the Loftons with arrest for truancy and an involuntary transfer, Americans for Family Values intervened on their behalf. We won the right to transfer Robert and his brother to a safer school, though it meant a long bus ride for them.

The Loftons' case is not unusual. I went through a similar situation with my own son, Troy. For a time I had him in daycare and private school. Like most parents, I wanted what was best for one of the treasures of my life. But Troy's friends went to public school, and he wanted to join them in junior high. Around the corner from our house was Audubon Junior High, which was considered one of the best schools in the black community.

The year was 1984 and Jesse Jackson was running for president. One of my son's teachers suggested that students write an essay on Jackson's candidacy. Troy wrote a paper criticizing the Jackson campaign. When it was returned, we found that the teacher had disdainfully circled certain items. Who had advised him? Whose thoughts were these? Troy's paper did have an occasional grammatical error, but he was singled out so unkindly that he started to become discouraged. In addition, Troy's assignments were mundane and trivial. He did his homework on the short walk home from school. Gangs were infiltrating the school. It was also known that Troy's mother was an activist. I was concerned. Like Linda Lofton, I wanted my child in a safer place with a greater academic challenge.

With the help of a friend, Eugene Fay, the principal of another junior high school, Troy was transferred to a school in Beverly Hills. In high school he was on the speech team, won awards, and got a job at an athletic club. He graduated from UCLA in 1994. I believe that Troy succeeded on his own because his father and I intervened in his education.

How many thousands of Roberts and Troys are there in Los Angeles and in cities all across the country? Their parents care about them just as much as Linda and I cared about our boys, but many of these parents are afraid to sound the alarm. If there's one thing I've learned, it's that change always involves risk. Are we willing to take risks to change—even save—our children's lives?

In 1993, the voters of California indicated they were not willing—yet—to take such a risk when they defeated Proposition 175, which would have provided for a system of school vouchers. This initiative faced a heavily financed campaign of opposition by the architects of the status quo. The same bureaucrats, unions, and liberal educational professionals who have given us schools that are saturated with weapons and unable to teach our children to read and do their sums warned the people of California that school choice was a threat to sound education. They won that battle, but they won't win the war. A parents' revolt is inevitable. I believe the day will come when parents have the right to choose the school that will best educate their child. As the old song says, "We shall overcome." The tragedy is that it might be too late for today's children trapped in the quagmire of third-rate schools.

One of the arguments made against vouchers was that public funds would be used to send children to religious schools. Of course, parents could have used their vouchers for *any* private school, religious or non-sectarian, but yes, most private schools are religiously affiliated. So what? Vouchers would have put California in line with virtually all the free nations of the world, which combine publicly supported education with the free exercise of religion as a matter of course. The United States is the only democracy that does not provide such funding.

During the California voucher campaign, Denis Doyle, a senior fellow of the Hudson Institute, wrote in the *Los Angeles Times*:

> Since 1971, with the Lemon v. Kurtzman *case, the Supreme Court has emphasized the "separation" clause, refusing to let public funds flow to religious schools. (The* Lemon *precedent sets out a three-part test for determining when a government practice amounts to an unconstitutional establishment of religion; conservative justices have long criticized the precedent.) By way of contrast, the Australian High Court*

emphasized the "free exercise" clause, and permits public funds to flow to any school, public or private, religious or secular, so long as the state is neutral and treats all religions—including irreligion—equally.

This is precisely what we do with health care and other social programs—babies can be born at public expense in a Catholic hospital; patients can be treated in Jewish, Methodist and Seventh-Day Adventist hospitals; the dead can be interred in hallowed ground at public expense; soldiers have access to chaplains (as do members of Congress, whose proceedings open with prayer); our coins proclaim "In God we trust" and the pledge to the flag refers to "one nation under God."[3]

I shake my head in disbelief as I look into the rearview mirror of my thirty-plus years in the schools. The decline in American education is real and alarming. Will this society let the agnostic scrupulosity of *Lemon v. Kurtzman* stop us from saving our schools?

In the end, school choice concerns more than just reform, badly needed as it is. It also concerns justice. As Mr. Doyle emphasized, "Poor youngsters who prefer a religious education are the nation's last unprotected minority; required by law to attend school, they have no choice—in America—but to attend a government school. In no other democracy are children so treated. Where is our moral and ethical response?"

PUBLIC EDUCATION, PUBLIC PROBLEM

Public education has a hidden agenda which makes it a very public problem. The way I was raised, we knew who was in charge. We went to school to learn. We may have come from impoverished neighborhoods, but we respected those in authority. Naturally, my upbringing affected the way I think today. Therefore, the philosophy and leadership moving our children into the twenty-first century will affect how they think and act in the future.

It was Easter 1994. My husband, Chuck, and I called the mother of one of his lifelong friends. She is a forty-year resident of Watts. We asked her if she planned on attending Easter services at her church. Her response was that there had been so many gunshots the night before that she was too exhausted to make the trip—even on Easter Sunday. This woman now lives in a war zone thanks, in part, to the modern public education we have dished up to the youth of our city.

Why do I say public education is a public problem? In order to believe with certainty, you must begin with doubting. I have sincere doubts about the educational system. It devalues America, it distorts history, it attacks free enterprise and religious faith. Too many teachers are ready to assert their civil rights but not to take responsibility for their students' learning. Multicultural fads buffet the curriculum while the basics are ignored. The public school system of Los Angeles attempts to teach in *ninety-six* languages. The system's priorities are completely confused: students read *The Color Purple* but the Bible is banned as literature.

People often say to me, "Ezola, we know what you are against, but what are you for? What are the answers? Is there hope?" Stay with me. There is hope. I have taken on the system and succeeded. It takes time and courage, money and volunteers, but change can happen.

JORDAN HIGH SCHOOL, WATTS

Black communities like Watts are liberal. That's what your television and your newspaper will tell you. Nonsense! Black Americans are much more conservative than their votes imply.

The struggle against the liberal tide that has marked my whole career began in the early '60s. I arrived in Los Angeles fresh from college, thrilled by the opportunities available in a "free" state. My first teaching job was at David Star Jordan

High School in Watts a couple of years before the infamous riots of 1965.

The aftermath of the riots was a turning point in my life. I saw taxpayers' money pour into the community expressly to educate our children and to fight crime. Then I saw how these funds were misused by the very politicians who today claim that America never cared about blacks because it never spent money on impoverished black children. That is a lie. The record shows that billions of dollars were spent on black communities after the riots. But black leaders want to preach the gospel of white America's callousness, a plain distortion of history.

Hitler understood in the 1930s that people will more easily fall for the Big Lie than for small ones. Nothing has changed. We ignore the real causes of our problems and pretend that they will go away with more government money. Meanwhile the riots of '65 gave way to the riots of '92. We never recovered from the former, and without heroic measures we will not recover from the latter.

Back at Jordan High School, I decided to make sure that public money devoted to education was used efficiently and honestly. Talk about an uphill battle! I never dreamed of the commotion I'd cause or the bruises I'd earn in this quest. But I was not born to be anyone's rubber stamp.

In 1976 I accepted the assignment of dean of girls, which made me responsible for the suspension of female students. It was then that I first noticed the blatant disregard of health codes, school board rules, education codes, and federal guidelines. In particular, I found that students were routinely being suspended for ten, fifteen, even twenty days, although the law set a maximum of five consecutive days. Moreover, their reinstatement was conditioned on a parent conference, again in plain violation of the law. The result of these practices was that students were dropping out of school in droves.

Following protocol, I complained first to my principal. For my troubles, I was demoted and transferred and lost my credentials. In 1978, I presented my allegations, along with charges of mismanagement, corruption, racism, patronage, and unethical, immoral, and unprofessional conduct, to

the Los Angeles Unified School District Board. If there was
ever an investigation of my charges, I never heard of it,
and I was not allowed to present evidence to the board.
Everyone, it seemed, knew about "the problems at Jordan
High," but no one wanted to do anything about them.

I pursued my complaint about the abuses and corruption
at Jordan for another five years. I brought it before the
school district, the district attorney, the state department of
education. Time and again the authorities ignored my
charges, refused to interview my witnesses, and "lost" the
records of wrong-doing. Meanwhile, who was minding the
children? Well, let me tell you.

The morning in June 1976 that my complaint about the
attendance policy was made known, word spread quickly
about "that Ezola." Then one morning in September, I found
that my name had been removed from my mailbox at
school. There was a new principal, the former one having
been transferred to another comfortable position. When I
asked him why I was not on the roster, he told me I was
transferred.

The first day of my new assignment, a security man
came in and walked around my classroom. I asked what he
wanted, and he told me that there had been a bomb threat.
Thereafter there were regular security checks of my
classroom. Then something nice happened.

The principal of my new school called me to his office.
He told me he had been warned that I was a troublemaker,
a rabble-rouser, a problem. That explained the extra security.
Then he leaned back in his chair and, with a warm smile,
said, "You are one of the best teachers I've ever had."

I was eventually returned to Jordan, but my welcome
wasn't exactly warm. They put me next door to another
teacher who had fought the illegal suspension policy. His
reward was a special education class, for which he had no
training. This poor man could not handle his students, and
my class was constantly disrupted by the deafening noise
emanating from the special-ed class.

Life in the "blackboard jungle" makes for some unlikely
friendships. Some gang members in the school decided they

liked me and called themselves my "protectors." They also took a liking to a terrified boy from the special-ed class who used to come to my room during lunch hour for shelter and quiet. The gang guys protected him too.

A few doors down was an art teacher who was also athletic director. Since he couldn't control the kids, he brought in football players to serve as "enforcers." They were rewarded with good grades.

Jordan High was not a school—it was a warehouse.

I finally transferred to another school. There my supervisor asked me for a reading list. I put the Bible at the top of the list. I was immediately called in for a conference and told I could not teach the Bible. I said that I was asked to submit a list of great books and that I had done so. He again told me I could not teach religion and again I replied that I was not. He backed off . . . then assigned me to teaching typing.

"Sin has many tools," says the book of Proverbs, "but a lie is the handle that fits all." All the money in the world won't fix our schools without truth. And there seems to be very little room for truth in the education establishment today.

Schools reflect society—an anxious society where kids are out of control, parents are out of ideas, and schools out to lunch. It's a situation where "sometimes you need Mr. Chips and sometimes you need Dirty Harry," remarked the former secretary of education, William Bennett. Disintegration calls for drastic measures. Some of these drastic measures are being taken in towns across America, with astounding results.

There is a restoration of principals with principles and of teachers with the determination to mold strong, law-abiding students, of safety and security, discipline and order, and an awareness of and respect for the law.

This hard line is not popular with the new slave masters. The American Civil Liberties Union fights schools that try to impose dress codes and discipline, even though the value of these things is indisputable. The "something-is-wrong-get-tough-about-it" approach does not play well with those who thrive on grants to "study the problem" again—and again—

and again. I see a new group of concerned Americans—parents—taking responsibility with their heads and hearts, at home and at school. And thank goodness. The time for business as usual at the Jordan High Schools of America is past. A society that can no longer be outraged is doomed.

CHAPTER 5
The Moral Imperative

"OH, MISS FOSTER . . ."

My students love to ask questions. They consider it a coup to stump, startle, or shock me. They are disappointed when I take everything in stride. I think they're actually grateful to have found someone who believes in absolutes, and so, though I pull no punches, they keep coming back for more.

"Oh, Miss Foster," they beg, "can't we talk about what you said on TV?" I insist that such issues be put on hold until our school assignments are complete. They know they are dealing with a no-nonsense teacher; when the bell rings, we get down to business. If there is no time to talk at the end of the hour, many students return during lunch break or after school to continue our conversations, which cover any issue they're concerned about—AIDS, abortion, rape, welfare, immigration, Martin Luther King Jr., school vouchers, civil rights, the future, poor grades, drugs—you name it. While I work to make learning a challenge, they think chatting and arguing with their teacher is much more fun. They don't realize that I'm just giving them a different kind of homework.

So much of what my students believe is a result of the current moral breakdown. These kids are street-smart, but they have none of the wisdom and understanding that comes from true debate, from listening to another point of view. Even at their young age, they have been indoctrinated with the "politically correct."

"Oh, Miss Foster, you're just old-fashioned. Everyone has sex before they get hitched. After all, sex is the only thing that's free!" Everyone? Free? I look shocked. "Not everyone," I firmly insist. I might point to the basketball star A.C. Greene and his policy of abstinence. They're dumbfounded.

They just can't believe it. I assure them that there are plenty of people like Greene, although the press prefers to glorify people like Magic Johnson. My students will confront me with the current acceptance of any and every way of life. Acceptance—"tolerance"—of every kind of behavior is the gospel preached to these children from the time they are in elementary school. The attitude of these children is exactly what I and so many other parents and teachers predicted when the current sex education programs, which are totally divorced from moral principles, were imposed.

When I was a young teacher, sex education first made its appearance in our schools ostensibly to prevent promiscuity and teenage pregnancy; the incidence of both has soared. Now there is AIDS education, which makes no pretense of encouraging chastity. Instead, the apostles of the sexual revolution have a forum for promoting homosexuality to our children. And *that's* going to solve the AIDS crisis?

The California State Board of Education unleashed one of these programs on elementary school children a few years ago, over the vigorous protests of Americans for Family Values and thousands of outraged parents. I knew that the majority of the black community would be appalled if they knew what the state was proposing to expose our youngest school children to in the name of "safe sex." This morally unhinged curriculum was approved anyway. I deal with the results every day.

"Oh, Miss Foster . . . ," goes the refrain, signaling the beginning of another debate on issues like these. This should not be surprising. Children learn best from example. The trouble is, they don't know a good example from a bad one. No one is teaching them moral imperatives.

"Oh, Miss Foster, my mom's boyfriend says you can't legislate morality." I respond, "Don't we do that all the time?" For a few moments the students consider what that means. I try to make it clear for them. Back and forth it goes: they hurl thoughts, shyly share frustrations, and repeat tales of "Guess who did this?" "Did you know . . ." "Listen to this . . . ." And I do listen intently, not just to the words, but to where the words are coming from. I feel it is important to give them both sides, and I bring in articles—not as propaganda, but to try to get them to think, to consider that there may be another way of looking at something.

There has been so much debate recently about morality. Is it my place to enter into it at school? The State of California seems to think it is. The state Education Code defines "Duties of Teacher—General" as follows:

> Each teacher shall endeavor to impress upon the minds of the pupils the principles of morality, truth, justice, patriotism, and a true comprehension of the rights, duties, and dignity of American citizenship, including kindness toward domestic pets and the humane treatment of living creatures, to teach them to avoid idleness, profanity, and falsehood, and to instruct them in manners and morals and the principles of a free government.

With this mandate, it is both a duty and a joy to offer guidance on the moral issues that affect these children. A friend refers to these as "code blue" issues because they have life and death consequences. One thing is sure. My students, and anyone else who listens, know where I stand. When was the last time you heard a member of the American black leadership take a stand on a question of morality?

Most of the students I see are in a moral Never-Never Land. People are either moral, immoral, or amoral. The latter simply have no sense of morality; they don't know or care one way or the other. There are a lot of people like that nowadays. I try to focus on children who have fallen into immorality. These are the ones we much reach. Many kids think they are moral, yet promote immorality, deforming the consciences of those who don't know the difference.

Liberals label people who believe as I do the "intolerant religious right." Coming from where I do, I am used to being labeled. The label is part of a strategy to lock us up in our churches and synagogues in the hope that, like old soldiers, we will just fade away.

I will not fade. The color of my skin is set. I will not retreat; advancing is more my style. I am armed with a moral mandate.

Most researchers, whatever their religious beliefs, now agree that crime originates, for the most part, in homes where there are no moral absolutes, no standards, no training. Since much of the formative years of our children is now left to daycare workers, instruction in what is right and wrong is often missing. Hard-working parents, at the end of a long day, may try to instill values in their children, but those children spend so much time in the presence of other influences that their parents' efforts may be futile. The Founding Fathers took it for granted that the democracy they established could not survive without a consensus about what is right and what is wrong. The failure of conscience that I witness every day is a deadly threat to our very survival.

The new morality—one without family, without objective standards of right and wrong—has no future. Until we recognize that, prisons will continue to overflow, innocent bystanders will continue to be victims of drive-by shootings— in short, our problems won't get one bit better. Stopping the calamitous cycle of immorality, violence, and broken lives won't be easy, but each of has to start right where he is. My part—and the part of every parent and teacher—is to encourage honest discussions with young people, and that starts with the old refrain, "Oh, Miss Foster."

WHO'S RIGHT?

Individual rights! Human rights! Civil rights! Inalienable rights! Gay rights! Is there no end to this interminable parade of rights? People who pursue their rights, inalienable as they may appear, forget who picks up the tab when those rights are abused.

The beating of Rodney King was deplorable. But I cannot help thinking that the outcome would have been entirely different had King acted responsibly and stopped when the police told him to. Those police officers did not go out looking

sister and I with our mother. She raised five children by herself on eighteen dollars a week. "The harder you work, the luckier you get."

With friends in Houston. I'm the one in the white cowboy boots.

e church my grandfather built in Maurice, Louisiana. Black people could sit in the front ws of this church. Sadly, though, houses of worship are still segregated in Maurice.

With the late Senator S.I. Hayakawa of California. This plain-spoken educator who becam
respected statesman late in life had no tolerance for liberal claptrap.

th my husband, Chuck, and the former Los Angeles chief of police, Daryl Gates. Amerians
Family Values rallied to Chief Gates after the Rodney King incident.

With my friend Hattie Frazer and Pat Buchanan. I told Pat that many people are convin
that he is less conservative than I. "Impossible!" he laughed.

h Bruce Herschensohn (left), a radio commentator and 1992 Republican senatorial candi-
e, and former mayor Sam Yorty of Los Angeles.

The men of my life: my husband, Chuck, and my son Troy.

for a black man to beat up and just happen to pick Rodney King. At the beginning of their encounter with Rodney King, they were doing their job as they were trained to do. I supported our police throughout that tragic episode because I believe they have rights too. I certainly want "the force" with me when my neighborhood is terrorized.

King originally asked for over fifty million dollars to compensate for the violation of his rights. However the case is resolved, the term "rights" keeps insinuating its way into our lives, often in a most inappropriate way.

Reginald Denny was also beat up. He was innocently doing his job when a mob, supposedly incensed over the verdict in the Rodney King case, dragged him from his truck and nearly killed him. The idea that, in a civilized society, people can be excused for such savagery because they were angry is ludicrous. What happened to the rights of Denny and the other law-abiding citizens who came under attack during that outrage?

Dr. Walter E. Williams analyzed the exculpation of Denny's assailants:

> From all outward appearances, the jury that acquitted Henry Watson and Damien Williams of most of the serious charges in the merciless beating of Reginald Denny during the '92 riots—seen numerous times on TV—acted in accordance with the sentiment of protest groups.
>
> Groups such as the Young Communist League, Free the LA 4 plus the Radical Women demonstrated outside the court chanting, "No justice in the courtroom, no peace on the streets." If that sentiment played a role in the jury's finding these two barbarians guilty of lesser charges, it is a sad day for racial relationships in Los Angeles and perhaps America.
>
> The jury's decision reminds me, a 57-year-old black man, of the judicial system of the Old South. There was little or no chance that a white jury would ever find a white person guilty of murder or rape when the victim was black. Black people rightfully protested against that kind of injustice. Indeed, that's why

> *Congress enacted the law whereby the U.S. attorney
> general could bring civil-rights charges against
> defendants who, because of the local climate, weren't
> found guilty of heinous crimes against blacks. We've
> witnessed the same injustice in the Reginald Denny case,
> with a difference in colors.*
>
> *From a social viewpoint, the Denny case has far
> broader implications. Whites don't have a monopoly on
> racism. In my opinion we'd all do well to review and re-
> evaluate the people who say they speak for blacks.*[4]

The civil rights movement seems to be taking a more
militant turn. Making heroes of hoodlums is beyond my
comprehension. Could it be that those who were shouting
so loudly were simply using the occasion to further their
own agendas?

Individually, I won't give up on gang members. Some of
them have been part of the "Oh, Miss Foster" group and
have acted as my bodyguards. But my stand on "gang
diplomacy," which gives gang members rights that are
denied their victims, is clear. In 1988 I addressed the problem
over the radio:

> *South Central Los Angeles has been plagued by gang
> activity for decades. During the Watts riots [of the 1960s]
> the most prominent hoodlums and looters emerged as
> the "new leaders" of the black community, received
> billions of tax dollars for job training programs, social
> welfare, and special education.*
>
> *More than twenty years later, South Central Los
> Angeles is worse off than before. Our own black leaders
> are sending the wrong message to our children, that
> killing, robbing, and mugging will be rewarded with more
> job programs and specially-funded government projects—
> as their right. A right to be rewarded for killing and
> looting and endangering lives.*
>
> *Let's address the real problem. Educate our children
> instead of establishing a police state in South Central
> Los Angeles.*[5]

The return of rioting in 1992 bitterly proved my point.

The "rights" of the relentless tide of illegal immigrants and drug-users, coupled with the failure of our public education system, have wreaked havoc on our black children. Why are the wrong rights perpetuated and the rights set forth by our Founding Fathers dismissed?

Each morning, as I sip my coffee and read the morning newspapers, I read one account after another of someone's rights being violated. Some are as inane as the suit brought by a woman against her employer because the air conditioning at work caused her such "pain and suffering" that she had to leave her job. A jury awarded her damages because of the insensitivity of her employer. I wondered why she didn't just move her desk or put on a sweater. Simple common sense solutions and communication are in shorter supply than I realized.

I see our black leaders hailing the rights of those who invade our borders. I see homeless people littering the sidewalks of our cities, using them for bedrooms and bathrooms because they have a right to sleep and live where they choose. I see fifteen-year-old girls having their second abortion because that's their right. Where did responsibility go?

Rights-mania has warped our expectations in life. We seem to think that the individual rights enshrined in our constitution are a guarantee of happiness.

THE CRISIS OF RESPONSIBILITY

I can't define another person's values, but I will not let anyone corrupt the values I have embedded in my heart. A lot of liberals are trying to do exactly that by taking advantage of some tragic crises to spread the poison of immorality and irresponsibility. It takes particular courage to tell the truth about AIDS, abortion, and other scourges, but the stakes are too high for us to be silent.

There are indicators that a global AIDS epidemic is looming. The World Health Organization predicts that there will be forty million HIV-positive persons by the turn of the century. What has been the response to this horrific threat?

Not a return to responsibility. Incredibly, the response of government, schools, foundations—almost every entity that could be expected to help end the crisis—has been to promote the very behavior that induced the crisis. The plague that should have sounded the death knell for the homosexual movement (and perhaps the rest of the sexual revolution) has instead propelled it to unheard-of levels of "public" (read government and the liberal media) sympathy.

The panacea that liberals offer (besides spending more money) is irresponsibility itself disguised as responsibility— "safe sex." What it really means is *more* sex, preferably with someone who is not your wife or husband. The conquest of school curricula coast to coast by the homosexual agenda, under the banner of safe sex, is nearly total. AIDS activists have pushed decency, morality, and parents' rights so far into the background that virtually any kind of perversion can be taught to school children as long as it is in some way related to "AIDS prevention."

The power of the sexual revolutionaries is tremendous, and you cross them at your peril. In 1987 I was arrested in the lobby of the Anaheim Hilton after some Republican Party leaders objected to the literature Americans for Family Values was distributing, which accused our then-governor and other top Republicans of shunning family values in order to appease homosexuals in the party. I was charged with trespassing, disturbing the peace, and resisting arrest and was finally released on five hundred dollars' bail.

It was worth the struggle. I returned to the Hilton and won approval of a resolution that condemned state-funded AIDS "educational" materials as pornographic, as well as one calling for the prosecution of dial-a-porn operators.

Even churches have jumped on the safe-sex bandwagon. Instead of teaching Christian virtue and responsibility, many of them accept government grants to teach homosexuals to indulge their passions "safely." No wailing from the liberals about separation of church and state here! They don't need to worry—biblical precepts about human love and procreation have no part in these churches' AIDS programs.

The American people and their democratic government have always considered homosexuality wrong, but it wasn't something we talked a lot about. Suddenly, homosexuals have "come out of the closet" and straights have been pushed in. I see it often when I am making a public statement. Someone like the cameraman I described at the beginning of this book will slip over and tell me how glad he is that I am speaking out for what is moral.

Many of those who embrace this "lifestyle" are now teaching in our schools. In many walks of life, it is becoming something of a badge of honor to be a homosexual, especially in the entertainment world. The same is true with respect to sexual immorality in general. We used to assume that most of our youngsters were virgins. But the last three decades have seen the old values so overrun by those advocating promiscuity that it's difficult for young people to take a stand.

Mother Teresa of Calcutta, speaking at the 1994 National Prayer Breakfast to an audience that included the president and vice president of the United States and their wives, said something astonishing about "unwanted" children. It was astonishing because so often a girl who is pregnant and unmarried is led to believe that she has no alternative to abortion.

Mother Teresa said: "I am willing to accept any child who would be aborted and to give that child to a married couple who will love the child and be loved by the child." She softly pleaded for "unwanted" children to be placed in adoptive homes. From her Calcutta headquarters she had placed more than three thousand children in adoptive homes. She answers the question of who will care for the babies if abortion is again outlawed. As Cal Thomas, a conservative commentator, points out, "Now the question is whether a woman contemplating abortion wishes to be selfish or selfless, to take life or to give life."

Is there any hope of righting today's crisis of responsibility? Yes. First we must challenge those in the classroom, the newsroom, and, yes, even the pulpit, to change their message. It's time we started teaching our children about their responsibilities, not just their "rights." Part of growing up is learning that actions have consequences. There's nothing new about that. Every generation has had to learn it, and this one can too.

"Oh, Miss Foster, when it comes to sex, we are only human." No one said you weren't. And as to the proverbial "we have rights, too," no one said you didn't. But don't fool yourself that the odds are in your favor in the sexual revolution. The apostles of "safe sex" don't necessarily have your well-being in mind. Americans for Family Values opposed a plan in California to distribute bleach kits and condoms to drug addicts on the street, arguing that it would encourage drug use. People like us—black people who believe in right and wrong—have had some success, even though you will seldom hear about our victories. The plan was defeated and we were elated that peaceful protest, armed with facts not guns, can work.

MAGIC WORDS

Asking, "What's missing from the news of Magic Johnson's plight?" Howard Rosenberg of the *Los Angeles Times* reminds us that we "saw his wife, friends, colleagues . . . , people with shock on their faces and pain in their eyes . . . , experts on medicine, sports, advertising, public policy, sociology . . . , AIDS activists and safe-sex activists. Chastity activists were missing."

How right he is! As if to prove the point, alongside Rosenberg's column the *Times* ran Rick DuBrow's asking, "How can the hypocrisy that buries condom ads on TV continue after Johnson, warned repeatedly about safe sex, indicated that he would carry the message to young people?"[6] Magic himself said that he "wants to become an educational spokesman on the virus." The headline in the business section read, "Sponsors May Use Magic in Ad to Encourage Safe Sex."

"Safe sex." So now those magic words are Magic's words. But how *safe* is it? Some people don't want parents and their children to know. The only major study of the effectiveness of condoms in preventing the spread of HIV was undertaken at the University of California at Los Angeles. Although thirty out of thirty-one brands passed an "inflation" test, 40 percent of the condoms failed a test to measure water leakage. You might have expected these results to occasion a rethinking of the whole "safe-sex" agenda. Instead, federal funding of the study was abruptly cut off. It has been said that a zealot is someone who, when confronted with irrefutable evidence that he is wrong, persists in acting according to his old ideas instead of in accord with the facts as they have been proved to be. The condom-pushers fit that description to a T.

Even if only three condoms in a hundred failed, I wouldn't accept the risk. If only three airplane passengers out of a hundred were going to die, wouldn't you want to know *which* three? Will I be one of them? Or someone next to me? Those odds are not good enough for the young people who come into my room looking for answers.

The abortion debate continues. The Supreme Court and abortion supporters tell us that women must have a choice. What do they mean by "choice?". Most young people lack the wisdom and experience to make the right choices in these life-altering dilemmas. They wake up one day to find that the act of pleasure has resulted in an embarrassing, unwanted pregnancy that could have been avoided.

I hear so few people talking about reproductive responsibility. Abortion is really the ultimate form of violence, disguised by the slogan of "freedom." What is it about "wait" our young people don't understand? There is always time to suffer the outcome of irresponsibility *after the fact,* but little time for reason before a crisis hits. Like children on a merry-go-round, the debate swirls round and round the facts, leaving almost everyone at risk. Sexual irresponsibility is a chief reason for high dropout rates in our schools and victimizes the frightened, reluctant mother as well as the father, who often performs a disappearing act.

The global epidemic of teenage pregnancy is not going away. I am convinced that "educating" by promoting condoms only encourages promiscuity. What is the real message of this advertisement, which ostensibly promotes responsibility?

> *I'm naked whenever I have sex. I might as well get naked again. What I have here is a condom, a latex condom. I wear one whenever I have sex. They stop the spread of HIV. I'm saying wear a latex condom if you're going to have sex. You can be naked without being exposed.*

As it happened, this ad was pulled in response to heavy protest—not because of its coarseness, but because it was discovered the rock star who recorded it had a long history of sexual battery. There are days when I want to apologize to my students on behalf of a society in which promiscuity is actually the subject of advertising.

In 1993 Americans for Family Values sought to bring rape charges against a Los Angeles high school basketball coach who had sex with one of his students, a fifteen-year-old girl. We were shocked by the reluctance of the authorities to pursue the investigation and the many attempts to protect the coach. This adult authority figure, a coach, a public servant, had abused the confidence placed in him by the girl's parents in the most appalling way. We wanted to help the family but to also to send a message to any teachers who might think of taking advantage of our children. The coach was placed on administrative leave pending the outcome of the investigation, and the case was finally dropped because the leading witness failed to appear.

We keep up the fight, working our way into the consciousness of those who will listen. The alternative is a society of moral illiterates. What scares me most is the growing number of people—kids and parents—who dismiss these problems with a shrug and the response, "People do it all the time."

So many of today's kids see no moral dimension to their actions. They are well versed in the "decision-making" techniques that crept into our educational system in the last few decades, but they can't make the fundamental decision of whether something is right or wrong. Dr. William Kilpatrick makes the case for traditional character education in his book *Why Johnny Can't Tell Right from Wrong*. He points out that character education "didn't ask children to reinvent the moral wheel; instead, it encouraged them to practice habits of courage, justice and self-control . . . . Decision-making curriculums pose thorny ethical dilemmas to students, leaving them with the impression that all morality is problematic; and that all questions of right and wrong are in dispute."[7]

What some call "values clarification" I call moral illiteracy. Having listened to "Oh, Miss Foster" for so many years, I am convinced that, by and large, our children are unequipped to make right decisions about morality. I will never forget that I have a statutory duty to teach morality.

BAD RAP

Negative values yield negative results. Newspapers and television have made the story of Ronald Ray Howard well known. He claimed that "gangsta rap" music influenced his behavior the night he shot a Texas state trooper. The episode shook the music industry, which has been putting disclaimers on those recordings ever since. Ronald Ray Howard's is not the only such case on record.

Rap music is the subject of considerable debate in America, but the debate is of special importance in the black community. The overwhelming majority of rappers are black, and they have a tremendous influence on our children.

The retail giant Ross Stores recently published back-to-school newspaper inserts featuring elementary school children wearing "gangsta rap" fashions—overalls, baggy pants and shirts, bandannas, and crooked baseball caps.

Rap is used to sell everything from Adidas shoes to Kool-Aid. Since advertisers recognize the influence rap has on our children, it is important that we do also.

The origin of rap as a popular music phenomenon can be traced back to the Sugar Hill Gang's *Rapper's Delight* of 1979. That was the first rap song to reach *Billboard*'s Top

Forty. Following the success of this number, other rap performers began to attract attention. Most of their songs were innocuous, concerned with things like basketball and failed love.

At rap's inception, some performers even tried to maintain a positive image. Stanley Burrell, known as "M.C. Hammer" (now shortened to "Hammer"), one of the largest-selling rappers, proclaimed, "I set an example for poor kids today who like my music . . . . With music, I have become successful and happy." Another rapper, "Queen Latifah" (Dana Owens), known as the Queen of Rap, has been described by some academics as one of rap's most intelligent voices. Her message is simple: peace, love, and respect.

Unfortunately, the positive attitudes personified by these two performers have become the exception rather than the rule in rap music.

In 1989, the criminal undertones often present in rap surfaced with alarming force. The stage names rappers used and their scowling, violent performances called into question rap's legitimacy. With the NWA ("Niggers With Attitudes") album *Straight Outta Compton,* America was introduced to a new style of rap, "gangsta rap," which proved to be not only a questionable form of entertainment, but a dangerous one.

The themes of this new rap genre were selling drugs, shooting policemen, and engaging in abusive sex. These entertainers made no effort to present a positive image. On the contrary, they claimed to have used drug-dealing profits to start their own record labels.

Tracks like "Gangsta, Gangsta and Dopeman" glorify the drug dealer's life. In another song, the members of NWA brag about "shooting anyone in a blue uniform." Ice-T's "Cop Killer" contains the same type of anti-police message.

While most members of the black community are law-abiding citizens, songs of this ilk make us seem like a community of thugs. Today, this style of violent "gangsta rap" dominates the genre. If anything, the songs have become more violent and misogynistic than they were to begin with.

NWA's first album contained a song berating women as gold diggers. Another album not only berates women but advocates killing them in songs entitled "To Kill a Hooker" and "One Less Bitch."

When rappers are criticized for producing this garbage they respond as Ice-T did during the hoopla over "Cop Killer": "That's the way it is on the streets" or "You just don't understand." Pardon me. I guess I don't understand advocating murder.

The majority of mothers and fathers understand well enough the message these people are preaching to their kids and know that it is hateful and destructive.

At a time when their message is becoming more and more distasteful, these rappers have become associated with black leaders. During the 1992 campaign, the Reverend Jesse Jackson came to Sister Souljah's defense after she suggested that blacks take a break from killing each other to kill white people.

To the mainstream media, Jesse Jackson, Maxine Waters, and Willie Brown of the California legislature represent the views of all black Americans, and all three of these people have come to the defense of rap music. Within the black community, however, these figures are commonly regarded as out of touch with the majority of mothers and fathers, who want their children to grow up in a decent and safe America.

If these rappers were an isolated group of inner-city youth, the problem would not be the subject of a national debate. But with MTV constantly broadcasting their venomous words and images, these rappers have the national spotlight as representatives of the black community.

Rappers appear regularly in films and on television. Their incessant exposure sends a dangerous message to youth and to our community: the way to be successful is to scowl, sell drugs, and abuse women.

The defenders of the outrageous rappers will tell you that there is no proof that young people act out what they hear in rap, and indeed it is probably impossible to *prove* a connection between violent rap lyrics and violent behavior. But let's not abandon common sense. Kay Coles James of the Family Research Council writes, "Art and culture have reciprocal effects. What a society esteems or despises is reflected in its music, movies and television, books and fine art. These reflections, then, are pasted across billboards and newpapers, displayed in museums, blasted on radios and ultimately filtered into our society's collective psyche."[8]

Nathan McCall offers living proof of the connection between popular culture and behavior. When he was nineteen, he acted out a fantasy sown in his mind by the movie *The Godfather*. When another man insulted his girl friend, he gunned the man down in revenge. Today McCall makes the case convincingly that "gansta rap" is conjuring up the same sort of fantasy in millions of young men's heads. McCall doesn't think much of the excuse that violence was a problem before rap came along. "Gangsta rappers often defend their themes by saying they reflect reality. But the brutality they toast has not always been part of our reality. This is a case of life imitating art in the worst way."[9]

As right-thinking people who recognize a threat to our children, what are we to do? Our constitution gives the right to free speech to all Americans, no matter how ridiculous their speech may be. As long as there is money to be made selling our heritage down the tubes, rap will be available.

We may not be able to censor violent rap, but that doesn't mean we can't censure it. Parents and public officials have but one recourse: exercise our right to free speech with public commentary on the perils of any music or agenda that advocates killing anyone—white, black, Asian, or Hispanic, male or female.

REPARATIONS

A new wrinkle in the agenda of many black leaders and activists is the demand for reparations for black Americans. The basis for this claim is the compensation paid to Japanese-Americans who were interred during World War II. Why shouldn't the descendants of Africans sold as slaves in America be compensated for their "loss of culture and humanity?"

It's been more than 130 years since the end of slavery, but Robert Brock is not deterred from making the case for reparations. He wants "forty acres and a mule," and more, for himself and his black brothers. He also says that interest should compound from the time of emancipation.

Brock argues that Southern blacks were not *freed*, they were only *emancipated*. He recalls a fifty-year-old case of a black chauffeur who had married a white woman. When the man's wife died, he was not allowed to inherit her house. Brock points out, rightly, how violated that man must have felt by such an injustice. But it is a long jump indeed from the case of the dispossessed chauffeur to paying out billions of dollars because of the injustices of an earlier age.

Still the campaign continues to gather steam. Its proponents collect signatures for their petitions in churches, at political meetings—wherever they can—on the assumption that blacks have a "right" to reparations. The movement assumed cosmetic legitimacy in 1989 when Representative John Conyers Jr., a Democrat from Michigan, introduced a reparations bill in Congress. The economic impact of such a measure would be enormous, to say nothing of the difficulty of establishing who is actually a descendant of slaves. Thousands of Africans were brought to these shores before the establishment of the United States of America, and some who came here were not enslaved. There's another gap in the theory behind reparations, one that we easily forget—the shameful complicity of Africans themselves in the slave trade. Many African chieftains enriched themselves by selling their own people. To both buyers and sellers, the whole arrangement was merely a business proposition.

Quite frankly, I think that blacks are blessed to be Americans. The suffering of our ancestors under slavery is an ugly, tragic chapter of America's history, but I pray that they will rest in peace, and I thank them for enduring their pain. There is no place I would rather live than in America. Our past had a future—a future for us.

Let us not forget the courage of the black people who came before us. The first ones survived a horrific voyage, followed by years of bitter hardship. The dark night of slavery passed, only to be followed by Jim Crow. The fact that we have so many opportunities today is a tribute to our parents, our grandparents—and America. Those who now demand their pound of flesh remain the unwitting victims of slavery.

Reparations are not a moral imperative. They are a prescription for even more strife between the races, and the only ones who stand to benefit are those who are trying to ride the issue to power. Since when did we abandon the principle of individual responsibility in favor of collective guilt? The good news for restoring morality is that *what has been self-inflicted can be self-corrected.*

CHAPTER 6
Snake Oil Peddlers

In the towns of the Old West, the arrival of a peddler's wagon never failed to stir up excitement. With his wagon wheels kicking up dust, and perhaps accompanied by the sound of a calliope or hurdy-gurdy, the peddler would hawk his "snake oil," a help-all, heal-all remedy, always backed by rousing personal testimonies.

The image of the snake oil peddler comes to mind whenever I listen to the rhetoric of politicians, preachers, and other "black leaders" who kick up enough dust to obscure the truth while they haul in the money. Their help-all, heal-all remedies have been spectacular failures ever since they were introduced in the 1960s. Nevertheless, they push their snake oil with passionate speeches, relentlessly repeated, that stir the souls of their unsuspecting victims. The dust has yet to settle. In contrast to their predecessors, who unloaded their shabby goods then quickly got out of town, these modern-day silver-tongued salesmen have thoroughly infiltrated our communities, embedding their notions of rights without responsibilities in the minds of susceptible blacks—men, women, and our children.

I am convinced that many of the problems in the black community today have their roots in the turbulent '60s, in the agenda still promoted by the snake oil peddlers. I use that term because they are masters of the lie. Their earnest faces never crack a smile. They join hands with the faithful and look you right in the eye and sell a huckster's bill of goods without a twinge of conscience. The term fits both preachers and politicians whose stock in trade is a set of demands far to the left of the Bill of Rights. It is sad to have to include among the snake oil peddlers preachers, who have been called to spread the word of God, not a liberal political agenda. Too many sacrifice the permanent on the altar of the immediate.

POLITICIANS

Snake oil politicians flourish because of a crisis of competent, strong black leaders. The 1990s are a precarious moment in America. There is no shortage of examples from our own day of the destructiveness of racial and ethnic strife: Bosnia, South Africa, the Middle East, Rwanda . . . . We are fooling ourselves if we think it can't happen here. Already, home-grown and foreign-born guerrilla gangs terrorize our communities while leaders, coalitions, commissions, and the press keep "studying" new programs.

Strangely absent from all the discussions is the question of leadership. Could this be because there are so few qualified leaders who speak with a voice of moderation? There has been little real change for the better in the last three decades: crime, poverty, militancy, and hopelessness have only increased. Taxpayers, on the other hand, are crushed under the ever-increasing weight of the welfare state.

I realize that many of our leaders talk as if they have the same values as the entire community, but their talk is deceptive. It is difficult to tell whether they are singing from their heart or only lip-syncing lyrics to entertain the audience. There are awfully few deeds to match their words.

It is easy for these politicians to say they're for family, God, and good jobs. Most of them, however, are too busy organizing marches and lobbying Congress to fund more programs to push us ever deeper into dependency. They are completely out of touch with most blacks.

Polls can be confusing, and one reason for the staying power of many leaders is the tendency of blacks to vote as a bloc—the sense of being faithful to your race that serves as a challenge to stay united. Under these circumstances, it's easy for the "once a leader, always a leader" syndrome to set in. Jesse Jackson, Maxine Waters, and Louis Farrakhan are in for the duration. While their allegiance is supposedly to our people, their accountability continues to be elusive, especially to those of us who hold conservative views. In fact, the only accountability I can ascertain is to themselves and their "group."

It is appalling to see one of Louis Farrakhan's lieutenants cast such hateful aspersions on Jews and the pope. Only after heated, nationwide criticism did Farrakhan offer the limpest apology for the remarks made in a public forum. We see Jesse Jackson, Farrakhan, and representatives from the Congressional Black Caucus and the NAACP standing together in a show of solidarity. Now on the whole, blacks do not exhibit hatred toward other groups. Why, then, do these leaders settle for such a weak apology, unless it's an attempt to condone or overlook the transgressions of one of their own?

I wish everyone, after study and reflection, would ask himself if black power has lived up to expectations. Looking back over the last thirty years, one sees increasing urban violence. Following the assassination of Martin Luther King, many cities were torched. Out of those ashes rose "black power." We watched as that power was exercised in the election of black mayors and other officials throughout our land. These newly elected black officials—many of them outstanding, educated, and competent—carried the black-power agenda into office with them.

Where are their accomplishments? The promise of eradicating poverty is unfulfilled. There are more people on the welfare rolls than ever before, often two or three generations in a family. I know welfare mothers who say, in private, that their lives were better in the old days. What a sad thing to hear from a black woman!

A slogan that I read years ago has stayed with me: "Black power isn't created at the ballot box." While blacks have not got richer or safer, many of their leaders have.

Statements like this surely mark me as a radical—a title I already share with the "snake oil" set, though they would add the prefix "dangerous." It wouldn't be the first time. I *am* a radical. I told Pat Buchanan that many people are convinced that he is less conservative than I. "Impossible!" he laughed.

I have ruffled feathers even among my fellow black conservatives. I don't enjoy doing that, but I will speak up for the truth even if my friends sometimes don't want to hear it.

A short time ago, I spoke at a conference with the Reverend Wayne Perryman of Seattle. "Our children must be told the truth," I said. "They are not Africans, they are Americans. Just as one can worship only one God, one can be loyal to only one country." My remarks were warmly received by our listeners, but it was clear that Mr. Perryman did not agree. I pointed to the example of Michael Jackson— *another* Michael Jackson. The one I was talking about is a radio commentator in California and a white South African American. Most black American children don't know what part of Africa their ancestors came from or how many generations they have been in this country. When Mr. Perryman began his presentation, he looked directly at me and retorted, "Africa is not a country, it is a continent." I wanted to stand up and answer, "All the more reason to be more specific when you tell our children they are African-Americans!"

Yes, I am a radical, but I'm not the only one. At a conference of Senator Arlen Specter's Republican Majority Committee, which is deeply interested in attracting black voters to the party, I ran into my friend Star Parker, the former welfare mother. Without mincing words, Star denounced the committee's attempt to reach out to blacks while at the same time promoting abortion. Senator Specter, Tom Campbell, Maureen Reagan, and the other pro-abortion Republicans at the meeting got a radical earful they aren't likely to forget.

Liberals have their differences too, but they manage to confirm and endorse one another all the same. Their solidarity shows their total commitment to their cause, however ineffective that cause is. Zeal for the cause—that's what will allow conservatives to be radical yet stick together.

I was amazed by the reaction to Clarence Thomas's nomination to the Supreme Court. Polls consistently showed that a majority of black Americans were in favor of his confirmation. Because he was black? That may have been the deciding factor for a few, but the polls showed that

Thomas's popularity among blacks was due in large part to the perception that he stood for family values.

So why did the so-called black leadership line up behind Anita Hill? Why did the press never question the leadership's fitness to represent black Americans on television and in the newspapers? Why did they all so studiously ignore the family-values streak in the profile of black America?

It is time for a new breed of activists. Conservative blacks need to mobilize against a leadership that does not have our true well-being at heart. It won't be easy to overcome the ingrained assumption that all blacks are liberal, that all blacks are Democrats. It won't be easy to overcome the Big Lie that conservatives have sold blacks down the river. We must remind ourselves that it is not a sin to question the new slave masters. The freedom won a century ago carried with it the responsibility to maintain our character and decency, goodness and thoughtfulness. Let's get on with it and leave behind those who would hold us back.

My students tell me that I live up to my name because, when it comes to the black leadership, I "foster" independence. You bet I do. I wouldn't *think* of telling my students to look at the past only as a stumbling block. I tell them to look at it as a stepping stone to a better future. The avenue of success is paved with self-reliance, and the map is a vision of the future. But try telling that to the leaders!

I can't think of a single black *leader* before the 1960s. What I do remember are black *heroes.* When I was in college, a young black boy named Emmit Til was lynched somewhere in the South. Amid rising talk of unrest on our campus, someone wisely invited the Olympics hero Jesse Owens to speak.

He was wonderful. He came and said what was important for us to hear: keep working toward your goal. It isn't easy, but you can achieve it. He was quiet and calm when he spoke, but the force of his life was an example that we needed. He was the opposite of Stokely Carmichael, who stood with a clenched fist in the air. Jesse Owens put his hand out, reaching toward us all. He represented not black power, but empowerment. His was the power of the people of America to recognize what was wrong and then right it.

His message had nothing to do with rage or revenge, yet here was a man who, by the sheer strength of his character, had faced down Hitler. We looked up to him and beyond him to our dream.

My introduction to the black "leadership" also came in college. A few people were telling us then that the black movement was to help black people and that in order to do this we would have to get more blacks in government. I don't remember hearing anything about choosing men of good character who would be concerned for others; the only prerequisite seemed to be dark skin. People appreciate choice. People want truth. But the black leadership's strident voices are a magnet for young followers more interested in a cause than in the truth.

It hurts me to see how black people are treated like sheep. When his movie *Malcolm X* came out, the director Spike Lee called on black parents to keep their children home from school for a day to see his film about the slain black leader of the '60s. Americans for Family Values held a press conference to weigh in against that bad idea. Joseph Lowery of the Southern Christian Leadership Conference added his voice to our protest, but in doing so he betrayed the arrogant mindset typical of our leadership establishment. Lowery said that Lee had *no right* to make his request. The black leadership, he pontificated, would come forward to instruct the community and parents in what to do. This is what I call manipulation by the "new slave masters."

Of course, the black leadership aren't the only ones who influence the black community. There is also the press, overwhelmingly liberal and obstinately uninterested in organizations espousing moral truths. There is one exception, though, to the liberal media monopoly, and that is talk radio. Conservatives' domination of radio talk shows is a bitter pill for the liberal establishment. It is no surprise, then, that the rest of the media are ganging up—joined by the president of the United States—to silence conservatives with such snide slogans as "Hush Rush." Others, like Pat Buchanan and Gordon Liddy, are also targets. Muzzling conservatives who speak out is a favorite pastime of liberals.

They have even introduced a bill in Congress to require radio stations to give equal time to liberals whenever a Rush Limbaugh criticizes the president or other political figures.

What are they so worried about? It's that millions of voters are now listening and watching, voters who could turn this country upside down if they joined forces to "throw the rascals out" and reclaim our country. That is the ultimate danger to the cause.

Thus the liberals' attack on the bottom line, requiring equal time for any opposing viewpoint at no cost to the opposition. Presidents Reagan and Bush killed such legislation, but Bill Clinton's presidency has breathed new life into it.

The Founding Fathers were aware of the potential for such tyranny masquerading as fairness. That is why they gave us the First Amendment.

Winston Churchill wrote:

> *The only guide to a man is his conscience; the only shield to his memory is the rectitude and sincerity of his actions. It is very imprudent to walk through life without this shield, because we are so often mocked by the failure of our hopes and the upsetting of our calculations; but with this shield, however the fates may play, we march always in the ranks of honor.*

Again I ask, Has black power lived up to its expectations? Has the media's message of untrammeled individual "rights" without moral norms made anyone's life better?

I have said a lot about the black leaders of our day, and now I am going to name some names. A list of leaders who have led black people down the garden path to near ruin could go on and on. But I would like to talk to just a few of them, one-on-one. I wonder if they have ever considered, or even heard, the point of view that I share with countless other black—and white—Americans.

Jesse Jackson

If I could take a few minutes and have a coffee break with Jesse Jackson, there are several things I would say to him.

First, be honest with the people. Clearly state your agenda—in its entirety! What are your goals for this country of ours? In specifics, not empty rhetoric. What are your international goals? I want you to let the people know the truth about how money has been diverted from the children in our public schools. Have you ever evaluated the results of all those programs that you give such clever names to, like "Operation PUSH" and "I Am Somebody"? The Los Angeles Unified School District spent more than a million dollars on just one of those programs. Today, things are worse than ever.

How can you visit our schools, Jesse, see the needs of the children there—the crime, the war zone they live in daily—and continue to ignore them? I wonder why you call school voucher plans racist when it's poor people who would benefit most. Please come clean with the people, Jesse. Do you love America and the values on which it was founded? Are you pleased with your accomplishments and satisfied with the lives you have saved?

What about your choke hold on black communities, Jesse? I am puzzled by "One Voice—One People—One Vote." In the early '80s you labeled *ABC Eyewitness News* as racist and personally led a widely publicized demonstration in front of the television studio. Though it was never publicly acknowledged, it was common knowledge among insiders that as part of the settlement, the network paid for ANC propaganda in *Time* magazine featuring Bishop Desmond Tutu, Nelson Mandela, and you.

Tutu, like Farrakhan, has warned, "there is going to be a race war in America." Tutu referred to President Reagan's "America First" speech as nauseating and said that "the West . . . can go to hell."

You curse the Reagan years, and yet that era saw many blacks rise to key positions. The media ignored the fact that during the Reagan Administration there were twice as many blacks in prominent positions as ever before. He signed legislation that added $25 million in funding to black colleges, 12 percent more than was spent under his predecessors. He received little credit for these actions, except from the future black lawyers, physicians, and businessmen who were educated by virtue of those expenditures.

So, Jesse, help me understand where you are coming from and your motives and your plan for a better America, and I'll buy the coffee.

Rosa Parks

Rosa, let's do lunch. We have a lot in common. I moved to the back of more buses than you can imagine, but there were times when I too wouldn't move back. Tell me your experience.

I would like our conversation to be private. Maybe at one of those old Greyhound bus depots where the seating area for blacks was delineated. I would like to look you right in the eyes, just the two of us, and ask what really happened on that famous day in Birmingham. There were many times when hard-working, tired-out black bus riders refused to move back—I know from my own experience—but no one took any notice. I wonder why. How come your refusal was so well recorded? How was it so quickly orchestrated? Were you really just a woman who happened to object when you were told where to sit, or was the episode carefully staged with your cooperation by your old friends in the NAACP?

Although many good things happened as a result of your famous bus ride, every time there is a celebration honoring you, it is used as a platform for saying something hateful about racist white America. Do you suppose *Hard Copy* or another one of those television shows would enjoy learning the facts behind the headlines?

It may take more than one lunch to share our stories.

Maxine Waters

Now that I think it over, this had better be a private conversation. In a public forum, you would shout me down. I've tried to reach you before, Maxine. In our quiet chat over a cup of tea, you could help me understand something that has troubled me since 1989. That year I found it necessary to file a complaint because some children from a housing project in Los Angeles were in danger. I helped a mother of ten transfer her children to a safer school. I will never forget your response. You decided that the best way to solve the crime problem was to "open a school within the housing project itself. If the children can't go to public school, provide one right in the project." (What about the school segregation that you're always criticizing?) Your proposal did nothing to make the project a safer place. I have so many more questions. How about recommending a quiet café somewhere in your district? Surely after your years in office, it is a safe place for two ladies to enjoy tea.

You support reparations for blacks. Maybe you should make reparations to the children of your old state assembly district, who have been poorly educated, mistreated, and have had to survive in a crime-infested neighborhood. Your old district has become a war zone, a killing field. Why hasn't it been cleaned up? You were in office for nearly twenty years. Those children deserve an apology.

We ran against each other on two occasions. I would suggest that while you won the election, the people lost. The downfall of Watts has aroused my determination to work for the cause that changes people and situations for the better. What accomplishments can you look back on with pride? How can your constituents look forward with hope? I am curious.

You worked for the telephone company before applying for a position with Head Start. Why is Head Start, to this day, just a baby-sitting service, offering nothing of substance? But you wore the title "teacher" well. You put a bandanna on your head and promoted a leftist agenda, working for those who were pleased to have you.

After all these years, Maxine, I ask you with pain in my heart, Why is your district a disaster area? Isn't it time for change? Give us an honest answer!

Americans for Family Values asked the teachers in your district a question, Maxine, and you might find their answers interesting. We asked them to define their primary function as teachers. Of those who responded, 58 percent said it was baby-sitting disguised as education. Teacher discouragement was at an all-time low. These are teachers in *your* district, Maxine.

I see a way to change things, and I would like to share it with you. It consists of four simple truths:

- We are not African-Americans. We are Americans.
- Our justice system may not be perfect, but it's the best one in the world (your comments notwithstanding).
- Public-school education is free; go to it and get it. It may not be great, but the kids in your district could succeed if given half a chance and taught the Three Rs (which don't include "racism").
- Teach children to work hard and develop good character. And remember, example isn't one thing . . . it's everything!

Nelson Mandela

My personal talk with you, Mr. Mandela, would be a solemn affair. I might be a bit fearful. I hope you could quiet my fears about the future of South Africa. I would like our meeting to take place in my small home. I would tell you what America means to me.

First I would like to ask you what your former wife, Winnie, meant when she repeatedly said that Africa would be freed with the "necklace." Why did it take you so long to speak out against that evil device? Most Americans think a necklace is something you buy in a jewelry shop, not a tire store.

The victims of the inhumane necklace treatment were township officials, black policemen, informers, or anyone else accused of working with the "system." They were dragged before a "people's court," presided over by radical black youth. No proof was required, a simple denunciation was sufficient. The trial was short and the guilty verdict foreordained.

The terrified victim's wrists were wired together. Then a tire was placed around his neck, filled with gasoline, and set on fire. The burning tire quickly reached five hundred degrees. As the rubber melted and ran down the victim's neck and torso, it burned deep into his flesh. At this stage the tire could not be removed, and the fire could not be extinguished with water.

It took up to twenty minutes for the victim to die. As he staggered in agony, the "comrades" laughed and jeered. The purpose was not just to kill, but to terrorize the onlookers and intimidate them into abject obedience. I quote your former wife, "Together, hand in hand with our boxes of matches and our necklaces, we shall liberate this country."

I also would like to ask you about your visits to Libya. When you were in Tripoli, you called Libya's ruler, Moammar Kadafi, a "comrade in arms." You thanked him for helping to train ANC fighters and condemned the U.S. air raids on Libya.

As a guest in Kadafi's Bedouin tent you said:

> You have given military training to South Africans who wanted to obtain their liberation through armed struggle. In our situation, as in other countries, an armed struggle is one of the most effective ways for fighting for political change in our country. Your readiness to provide us with the facilities of forming an army of liberation indicated your commitment to the fight for peace and human rights in the world.[10]

I know that you were reared in the same wealthy neighborhood as Chief Mangosuthu Gatsha Buthelezi, who was your friend. The two of you followed different paths to liberation and peace.

You say you "go in peace," but your words to Kadafi suggest otherwise—as does your association with Fidel Castro. In America, a man is known by the friends he keeps. What are we to think about your friendships?

I know that you are a very intelligent man. America will be interested in the relations the new South Africa has with the likes of Arafat, Castro, and Kadafi. There are still many in America who look back with pride and forward with hope—hope and faith for peaceful change.

*   *   *

The tactics of Nelson Mandela and the African National Congress in South Africa are no different from those of Jesse Jackson and the Congressional Black Caucus in the United States. Black communities throughout America have fallen under the domination of groups like the NAACP, the Urban League, Brotherhood Crusade, and the African Methodist Episcopal Church. By means of propaganda and intimidation, members of the community are made to submit to rules established by those leaders.

The ANC has made it clear to all the world that it is the only voice of the entire black population of South Africa. The Zulu nation is the last source of opposition to the ANC's complete control. Chief Buthelezi of the Zulus believes that his people have the right to remain free and independent. It is due in large part to the influence of the Congressional Black Caucus that Nelson Mandela received the political and financial support to consolidate his power. When the NAACP, Jesse Jackson, and Louis Farrakhan stand pat with the CBC, it gets its way.

No American, especially one of African ancestry, would want to be ruled by men who would adorn dissenters with a burning necklace of fire. Ask the people in Watts how they like living in a war zone.

In black America today, our intellectuals are often silent. Where is the moral sensibility that does not hide its face from evil? The fact that something doesn't feel wrong does not mean that it isn't wrong. You tell me that standards are in constant flux and that we need to accept the change. Whose standards have changed? Not mine! Is everything acceptable?

The Chinese character for "crisis" is a combination of the characters for "danger" and "opportunity." I fear that the snake oil peddlers have brought us to the brink of crisis. We have not heeded the warnings. May it not be too late to recognize the danger and seize the opportunity to act. Much more than just the black community is at risk. The threat is to America itself. The greatest loss remains the loss of truth and character.

PREACHERS

Louis Farrakhan

I'd like to have a private conversation with you. I prefer that the press not be present. I would like to speak heart to heart. Islamic countries are noted for their strong, aromatic coffee. I'd like to try some as an accompaniment for my likewise strong concerns.

Actually, I don't know if you would meet with me at all. I know that in the spring of 1994, you canceled an appearance at my alma mater because you did not want women in the audience. That makes me wonder what you think of women.

Is it true that you were an actor and entertainer? You are certainly a talented man, but do you put your oratorical skills at the service of peace or violence?

You have said that you are fighting for the freedom of all men. In the '60s I joined a fight for freedom. Then one day I realized that I was already free. It was now up to me to maintain and extend that freedom. What are you really fighting for? Is it freedom, or is it power and control? I worry that corrupt politicians and preachers are misleading the community. They keep the flames of racism burning rather than focusing on more positive goals. Our children deserve better.

When your lieutenants uttered those ugly words about the Jews, I was confused because in the eyes of many blacks the Nation of Islam embodies what is best in our people. Did those statements reflect your own opinion? I couldn't tell from your apology. Fortunately, there was some censure, but why do you remain silent while such ugliness is spewed?

I have demonstrated before. As a black who grew up in a segregated southern town, I participated in Martin Luther King Jr.'s sit-ins to bring about integration. I shared Dr. King's dream of seeing all "our children walk hand in hand through this land of opportunity." But I see now that this dream will never become a reality as long as there are black leaders who refuse to speak out against hate, racism, and anti-Semitism when the messenger happens to be black.

With so many blacks willing to drink the poison that men like you pour out in your thirst for power, we need leaders who will denounce your manipulation of our youth. Yet there they were, all lined up beside you in a show of solidarity: Jesse Jackson, Congressmen Kweisi Mfume and Maxine Waters, and Ben Chavis of the NAACP.

If you black leaders won't stop running toward the wrong goal line, then it is time for you to stop carrying the ball for us. How can we be silent? I have never relied on silence as a way to right a wrong. That's why we're having this discussion. The wounds you have inflicted are deep, and the bleeding has not stopped.

Hatemongers come in all colors, and bigotry knows no boundaries. How much territory are you after, Mr. Farrakhan? How far will you go to silence those who are dangerous to your cause?

Forgive me for not finishing my coffee. Besides, it isn't your style to listen to women anyway, is it?

Martin Luther King Jr.

What would you think, Dr. King, of those who represent black people today? You believed in nonviolence, yet you said that had you been a German under Hitler, you would have risen up against him. Would you stand up to some of the black leaders of today? Would you have spoken out against the hate that spews forth from their mouths? It is hard for me to imagine your lining up with Maxine Waters and all the rest in support of Louis Farrakhan.

Your dream of racial equality has not come as far as some suggest. There are more black leaders today than when you died, but our people still suffer from illiteracy and unemployment. What would you think of the black leaders who scramble after fame and power over the backs of their less fortunate brothers and sisters? I must tell you, sadly, that your dream has become a nightmare.

It became a nightmare at a school in Wisconsin when your birthday was not observed as a holiday. Angry black students protested by bullying white students, calling it "white kill day." This in remembrance of a man who preached nonviolence?

Your own words put them to shame: "Every man must be respected because God loves him. The worth of an individual does not lie in the measure of his intellect, his racial origin, or his social position. Human worth lies in relatedness to God. An individual has value because he has value to God."

You once said in a sermon, "*Agape* is not a weak, passive love. It is love in action. It doesn't stop at the first mile, but it goes the second mile to restore community. It is a willingness to forgive, not seven times, but seventy times seven to restore community. The cross is the eternal expression of the length to which God will go in order to restore broken community."

Is reconciliation possible in the shattered inner cities of our country? I believe you would still respond, "I believe that unarmed truth and unconditional love will have the final word and reality. This is why right temporarily defeated is stronger than evil triumphant."

I believe, Dr. King, that you would share my pain over the state of black America. But as I pay tribute to your memory, I take heart from your words, and I join you in the joyful cry, "We shall overcome!"

CHAPTER 7
Ebony in Agony

BEIRUT, U.S.A.

Welcome to Watts—or as *U.S. News & World Report* has called it, "Beirut, U.S.A." The riots that devastated Watts in the '60s were attributed to resentment of Jewish merchants and police brutality. When it happened again in 1992, the cause was supposedly Korean merchants and police brutality. Not much has changed, has it?

For almost twenty years, Watts has virtually been the property of Maxine Waters, its representative first in the state assembly and now in the U.S. Congress. *Ebony* magazine calls Maxine the most powerful black woman in America. What is life like in her district? From time to time, children pass dead bodies on their way to school. They have to take time out from learning to attend "grief classes." Going out at night means dodging bullets. In short, it's a war zone.

There are still some people who don't take the situation seriously. A case in point is Willie Brown. He is the speaker of the California House of Representatives. He is black. A few years ago he told an audience of criminal defense lawyers that they should organize their clients into a lobbying force against law-and-order advocates. He promised that lawmakers would listen. "I don't know any legislator up there," he said, "who doesn't have somebody in his family who has violated the law."

Maxine and Willie fiddle while Watts burns.

The children living in Beirut, U.S.A., are repeatedly told that white America is racist and that Africa, not America, is their homeland. One mother told me in a hushed voice, "I wish I could vote for a Republican, but unfortunately I'm not rich." She was serious.

Violence once erupted in a New York high school between black and white students when the blacks refused to salute the flag. In most of the schools in Watts, there isn't even a flag to salute. But there are graffiti-covered signs with the admonition "Leave your guns at the door." Our children are lost. They aimlessly walk the streets and learn to duck for cover at the sound of gunfire, unless their parents have shut them up in their house for safety.

I am often asked if I think there will be another riot, or even a race war. The Los Angeles police feared just that as they awaited the verdict in the second Rodney King beating trial. They assembled a massive show of force. The National Guard was also on hand, and SWAT teams took up strategic perches throughout the area. Mounted officers patrolled the streets. One lady noted that for the first time she felt safe. But what a price. Let's not forget that safety is her right. Another riot? It seems inevitable.

Who benefits from a riot? In 1992 it was gangs like the "Crips" and the "Bloods." Members of these gangs have appeared on the *Donahue* show, and some attended the inauguration of President Clinton. They got into the spotlight and loved it. Recalling the riot, one gang member said, "Yeah, we drove by. We killed a few people. But ya know, we've changed now. We've reformed." I was taught that killing is a crime that demands retribution, but here was another gangster who had beaten the system—if you can call it a system.

The gang members are not the only ones to exhibit this failure of conscience. Alice Harris, the highly publicized founder of Mothers of Watts, is often pictured holding a fan she took from a store in the looting that accompanied the '65 riot. Her explanation: "We weren't criminals, we were just family folks. We knew it was going to burn anyway, so why not get what we could?" She kept her spoils. She tells of going into a dress shop and being disappointed that it was already "picked clean." She wanted to "get me some of those dresses." Rummaging through the broken glass, she spotted the fan.

She excused her actions by saying that blacks had suffered from high prices and poor merchandise. This was the community's chance to get even. Unfortunately, her message is not lost on the youth of our community.

A couple of days after the '92 riot I debated a civil rights activist on television. We agreed that we are fighting a war, but we did not agree on when it started. According to my opponent, it started back with slavery. I asked her if that meant we are doomed to a perpetual state of war since we cannot do anything about the past. I suggested that we need go back no farther than 1984, when Louis Farrakhan, whom Jesse Jackson's presidential campaign had just brought to national attention, predicted a race war in America to be fought by young black gang members.

What was the response to such nonsense? Nothing. In the brotherhood of black leaders, everyone understood that Farrakhan was merely engaging in showmanship, as they all do. They are interested not in instilling responsibility and worthwhile values in our youth but in putting on a show. Their success is measured not by how many young lives they turn around but by how many television cameras show up at a press conference.

Danny Bakewell of the Brotherhood Crusade once enlisted Jim Brown, the former football star, in a campaign to exonerate a gangster who had served six years in prison for second-degree murder on the contrived theory that the police had framed him. Another victim! After this young man was released, he attempted to rob a pawn shop, yet Bakewell and Brown took pride in parading him around the city, passing him off as a hero. Although this "hero" had been tried and convicted, his patrons circulated petitions for his release and collected money for his defense, all as part of a campaign to "take back our community."

Take back our community? From *whom*? These leaders need to think about whose side they are on.

I cannot imagine anyone much poorer than my family was when I grew up. Yet no one in our little pocket of poverty ever dreamt of burning down somebody else's place just because he had something we didn't. And even though we suffered from much more racism than most of these young gangsters today, we always had hope and a vision that we could and would do better, that there was something we would accomplish, no matter the situation. Poverty was never an excuse. That was ingrained in us by our schools, teachers, clergymen, and families. This is not what our leaders are telling our young people today.

Will there be another riot? I wish I knew. It depends on how badly the gangs want the money and the leadership wants the recognition. Meanwhile, a frightened child comes to school with dark circles under her eyes. She had seen a trail of blood in the street the night before, and she couldn't get the piercing sound of gunfire out of her head as she tried to sleep. She's only nine years old. Danny Bakewell thinks the *police* are her enemy.

THE ENDANGERED BLACK MALE

Environmentalists are more diligent in protecting the kangaroo rat or popcorn shrimp than our black leadership is in protecting the endangered black male.

The statistics for young black men in the United States are grim:

- One out of four is in jail or on probation or parole.
- Violence is the number one cause of death between the ages of fifteen and twenty-five. The murder rate is ten times higher than that for whites.
- Black men in the inner cities are less likely to live until they are sixty-five than men in Bangladesh, one of the poorest countries in the world.

The anecdotal evidence is just as bleak. One young man proudly displays his belt, which bears more than seventy notches, representing the times he has "scored" with a girl, some as young as eleven. "Who knows how many kids I have runnin' around the project, or how many times my women get them thwarted?" He means aborted.

There is the thirteen-year-old boy with the face of a fifty-year-old, doing time for robbery and cocaine.

Another black youth, in prison for life, says, "The young men I grew up with are dead, incarcerated, or born-again Christians. A few got nice jobs but a lot don't have that opportunity."

Ghetto kids wonder why they should bother with five-dollar-an-hour jobs when they can make hundreds of dollars selling drugs.

Grim as these stories are, there are a lot of enterprising young blacks who are making it in spite of the odds. Somehow they have avoided the "What have you done for me lately?" attitude and have learned that the harder you work, the "luckier" you get.

Tom Sands, who has moved his family from inner-city Detroit to the suburbs, recalls how he was jolted out of the old way of looking at things:

I acted like a victim. I was a victim. I was hurt by society, education eluded me. My parents could not care less. The political system offered me food stamps. I was surrounded by racism and sexism, but I walked out of it. How did it happen? Someone handed me an editorial, copied rather crudely, but it made a lot of sense. It read:

I don't need to learn or to benefit from my mistakes—I haven't made any.

I don't need to overcome any weaknesses—they aren't weaknesses, they are cultural influences that are an unfortunate liability for which I am to blame others.

I don't need to change, because, after all, that's me, that's my life style, and therefore it's legitimate not only for me but for everyone else to recognize and accept.

I don't need to give up anything. Rather, I need to demand more of my rights. And I will, wherever I am, in whatever situation I find myself. And if you or anyone else tries to stop me, you will be my enemy. I'll tell you to "get out of my face."

Tom Sands found his chance in a church in the inner city where values, hope, opportunity, and forgiveness were

still to be found. What does the church have to offer? Tom
Sands will tell you. A new beginning.

There are plenty of excuses available for a black person
who does not succeed: racism, bad education, inadequate
government programs—on and on. A new beginning starts
with oneself. I am proud of my husband, Chuck. He is a
shining example of someone's taking charge of his own
life. He did not have a good education; he never cracked a
book. No demands were made of him; he just drifted through
the system.

He wanted a better life. He would go with his mother
and observe the business while she worked for a drapery
manufacturer. Occasionally he had the opportunity to drive
the company truck, and he was so careful and diligent.
Hoping he would someday be hired on a permanent basis,
he began learning the Los Angeles streets and freeways.
The day came when he secured the job. He was praised for
the efficient way he scheduled and completed the trips.
Making the effort to learn his way around set him apart
from some of the others. He kept watching and learning.

While driving for the drapery company, Chuck always
arrived at work early and learned more than his job required.
Soon he got a job with a trucking company, where his good
work won him the friendship of the management group,
and he started playing golf with his supervisor.

One day he asked why there weren't more blacks working
for the company. The supervisor said he didn't know where
to find blacks who were good workers. Chuck said he did.
He gathered some of his friends and after hours, with no
extra pay, trained them to drive the large trucks. Eventually
they were hired.

Chuck did not need affirmative action or a government-
funded training program. He was self-sufficient and he grew,
pushing himself to stretch his capabilities. Chuck's story is like
so many I heard growing up. It is about doing a little more
than is expected. That's a work ethic few people have anymore.

Working hard and working well don't guarantee,
however, that you won't meet adversity, as Chuck learned
when the trucking company was sold. Overnight the

management changed and so did their attitudes and policies. Chuck used to come in every morning through the front door and have a cup of coffee with the bosses before starting the workday. The new management had other ideas. The first morning, Chuck was stopped at the door and told to come in through the side door with the other drivers.

A few months later Chuck was illegally fired. After filing a grievance for wrongful termination he was reinstated. Then in the heat of the summer he didn't wear a shirt under his overalls and was fired again. Another grievance and another reinstatement.

It soon became clear that racism was at the root of Chuck's mistreatment. When he insisted on observing Martin Luther King's birthday, he was fired. Later, the supervisor approached Chuck at a catering truck in the parking lot and said, "Is it is or is it ain't the coon's birthday?" Again we filed charges against the management and again we won, but racial slurs had become a daily reality.

It was during these difficult times that we really learned that we are responsible for ourselves. The NAACP and the Urban League were not there to help us.

Liberal civil rights organizations tell the black community that the legal system will not work for them. Chuck and I found the opposite to be true. We were not militant; we used the system the way it was intended to be used and we won. One thing is for sure, we never considered rioting or stealing.

When I debated Professor Pearl Cleage of Spellman College on television, she said, "Black men are going down and taking America with them." Not my husband! If Chuck had been less of a man, he would have walked out on that company a lot sooner. But right is right, and he was willing to defend it whatever the cost. Black men don't need others to speak for them. Black men can speak for themselves.

We make our own choices every day. No one is helpless.

CHAPTER 8
There Is Hope

I can see myself now. A five-year-old girl with a skinned knee and pigtails crouched in a dark corner of our house. In a game of hide-and-seek, I'm impatiently waiting for one of my three brothers to "find" me. The anticipation of their footsteps is part of the fun. I listen intently while the mischievous boys move from room to room, pretending to be unable to find me. Playfully they call, "Ee-ZOH-la! Ezola, where ARE you? Ready or not, you're gonna be caught!" It was so exciting and reassuring to be found.

I remember other times when the bigger kids asked me to play hide-and-seek, then conveniently "forgot" about me. I remained hidden, but they stopped looking. My heart sank when their voices trailed off. Nothing was so sad as being forgotten in a game of hide-and-seek.

Life in the inner-city resembles that game. There are multitudes of people hiding in the dark corners of the ghettos and projects, anxiously waiting to be found. Their hope fades into dim reality.

"Hope deferred makes the heart sick, but desire fulfilled is renewal of life." "If we hope for that we see not, then do we with patience wait for it."[11] Our communities are in desperate need of a fresh, honest, lavish dose of hope.

Giving people a highway to hope is one of the joys of living and teaching in the same community, which can be challenging and exhausting.

On Mothers' Day a few years ago I received a call from a distraught mother, pregnant with another child. She told me that she could not get to work because her car was blocked by a mountain of illegally dumped trash. Her calls to the sanitation department, city hall, and her councilman were ignored. They passed her off as if she were another item on the rubbish heap.

I was outraged. The next morning I held a press conference in the woman's alley amid the filth and debris. The news coverage proved embarrassing to those who had turned a deaf ear to this woman's pleas, and the trash was hauled away. Although there were no consequences for the bureaucrats who had done nothing to help (business as usual), the pregnant mother was overjoyed. Her hope was restored in a small way. She reminded me that restoring hope is not just a privilege, it's a duty.

All over the country, I see signs of a resurgence of hope. We can pontificate all day on who is to blame for the dismal mess we're in (I have given you my opinions), but in the end, blame is like that mountain of trash: useless.

> *Blame never affirms, it assaults.*
> *Blame never restores, it wounds.*
> *Blame never solves, it complicates.*
> *Blame never unites, it separates.*
> *Blame never forgives, it rejects.*
> *Blame never forgets, it remembers.*
> *Blame never builds, it destroys.*

I am encouraged to see a growing movement to restore and revitalize family bonds. People are finally recognizing what a calamity the disintegration of our homes has been. Even some of those youngsters who, not so long ago, sashayed into my room with their skeptical "Oh, Miss Foster" have learned that the answers I gave them were true.

I rejoice in our victories, and I mourn that there is so much yet to be done. Ebony remains in agony. My husband and I drive through Watts, where we have spent so many years of our lives, and we see the gang graffiti and the fearful faces. I wonder if these people feel as hopeless as I did so many years ago waiting to be found by the bigger kids, who never came.

Hope sprang up recently in Jackson, Mississippi. At a public high school the student-body president had read over the intercom a six-second prayer modeled after the one used to open sessions of Congress. The students had voted 490 to 96 in favor of such prayers, and the principal, a black man named Bishop Knox, had given the go-ahead.

Mr. Knox soon discovered that he had walked into a hornet's nest. Battle lines were drawn in Jackson, and the principal was placed on administrative leave for having exercised "poor judgment."

Mr. Knox had relied on a 1992 decision by a U.S. court of appeals in Louisiana holding that student-led prayers were constitutional at graduation ceremonies. He was convinced that the prayer met the court's requirement of being nonsectarian and non-proselytizing.

Bishop Knox was fired the day before Thanksgiving of 1993. In his gracious response, he affirmed that obedience to his conscience was more important than a job. Supporting him were a host of students, including a ninth-grader who said, "We should have prayer in school, the law says freedom *of* religion, not *from* religion. They are violating the majority right to have prayer." Parents agreed. In a poll of the city, 97 percent thought that Mr. Knox should not have been fired. The case is still pending, although he has been reinstated.

His courage has given hope to thousands of others that some day prayer will be returned to the schools. At a rally on the Mississippi capitol steps, Governor Kirk Fordice said, "One day, I hope soon, it's not going to be legal to keep prayer out of public schools." Hope triumphed over adversity in Mississippi.

I have hope that black families will emerge from what I call an identity crisis and stand up for what they truly believe. The majority are good and proud people. They have been victimized by the liberal technique used by so many of our leaders: say the right thing, but propose the wrong solution.

Mason Weaver, the host of a San Diego talk show, gives an example of this: "The Rainbow Coalition [was] speaking out against black-on-black crime, which everyone knows is harmful and needs to be stopped. The coalition is good at identifying the problem but their answer was a call for more federal spending and rewarding criminals with college degrees."

Weaver continues, "The liberal thought process and training allows him [the liberal] to ignore facts and logic, he will deny the truth even when it is right in front of him . . . .

"They are going to claim the moral high ground, 'we are for economic improvement, against racism, and want better housing, etc.' I would suggest you totally agree with their goals and objectives but tactfully disagree with their solutions. The liberals have had thirty years to try their solutions and they just don't work (except for their pocketbooks), and it's time for new ones."

I see a multitude of rising conservatives. We are growing. If you tell the truth, there is no defense against it. And there is no shortage of role models. I think of General Colin Powell. He emerged from Harlem to lead our troops in the Gulf War. He became chairman of the Joint Chiefs of Staff because of his character and ability. Colin Powell is a genuine hero for our youth and a living lesson that a kid from an impoverished background can succeed.

Walter Williams reminds us that true success is color-blind, citing Bill Gates, the white founder and chairman of Microsoft. In their resentment of the success of people like Gates, Williams says, liberals get everything backwards. They "lionize thieves and criminals as victims of society," while at the same time vilifying the productivity of the rich. Instead of worrying about what Bill Gates is giving back, we should demand something back from the thief, who has produced nothing. "Bill Gates and his ilk have already served their fellow man by making life easier for us all and providing jobs in the process."

The first step we have to take is joining hands, black and white, not as hyphenated Americans but as *all* Americans. The second step is throwing out all the old excuses: place of birth, roots, early struggle, economic status. Sure those things are important, sure they shape our lives. But liberals think they *define* us. If we define ourselves as black or white, rich or poor, instead of just American, then we divide ourselves.

I want to challenge Americans, especially the young, to restore the ties that bind, the sense of family and community.

People ask me for specific solutions. Here are a couple:

- Cut the government programs that we know are ineffective. Redirect funding to those who will use the assistance as a bridge or stop-gap until they are able to be self-reliant.

- Reinvent the public education system and stop following the advice of the National Education Association. Under the NEA,the public schools in American cities have been changed into socialist training camps. "Diversity" and "multiculturalism" do nothing more than promote hatred for America and bigotry against other ethnic groups. America's public schools should be in the business of teaching American culture.

If I could reinvent the schools in Watts and South Central L.A., I would first toss out the "frills" classes such as "grief" and "sex education." Beginning in elementary school, the emphasis would be on reading and math. Students could not move up to the next grade without first demonstrating grade-level reading and math proficiency.

If I could reinvent the schools, each high school student would be required to take biology, chemistry, physics, algebra, and geometry, and he would have English grammar, composition, and literature every semester. American and world history, civics, a foreign language, and physical education would be required. Health and human reproduction would be covered in biology.

If I could reinvent the schools, we would say good-bye to peer counseling, sex counseling, and every other kind of nonsense counseling. Schools would not be free food distribution centers; we would rely on the churches for that. There's a Biblical mandate to feed the poor and clothe the naked, and there are many who willingly respond, working in the name of the Lord, not the name of another failed program.

If I could reinvent the schools, we would appoint administrators on the basis of merit, not patronage, nepotism, and favoritism. Our schools need good management. The business of running a school must be separated from the art and heart of teaching.

If I could reinvent the schools, students with behavioral problems would once again be taught at alternative schools, where they would not disrupt the students who are without such problems. That's how it was done when I started teaching, and it deterred crime while challenging the troubled students.

Profanity and obscenity, spoken and written, would not be found in the classroom. We would teach children to be more concerned about their manners than their rights.

And I'm not shy about saying that, if I could reinvent the schools, prayer would be restored along the lines that the heroic Bishop Knox tried to restore it. Our children are not animals but creatures with souls, made in the image and likeness of God.

Such a program requires fortitude. I have it. I hope the majority of my countrymen do too. If we work together, we can break the bonds of the new slave masters, we can run the snake oil peddlers out of town.

Many of my people have stopped hoping. They have accumulated enough of life's disappointments to be afraid to dream, to reach, to broaden their horizons, to dare to come out from the dark corners of hiding and risk being found. I want to shout HOPE from the housetops of the inner cities: "Ready or not you're gonna be caught"—caught by a future built on hope.

Britain's "Iron Lady," Margaret Thatcher, warned, "There is little hope for our countries if the hearts of men and women in democratic societies cannot be touched by a call to something greater than ourselves."

Let us join then, America, in answering that call, the call of a new day built on traditional beliefs. I am also challenging black America to believe that we are not just making another promise or playing another game. We can overcome the old obstacles to our hopes and aspirations. Yesterday ended last night! I believe a better tomorrow is coming.

Notes

[1] John Leo, "All the Rage," *Reader's Digest*, July 1993, pp. 135-136; originally published in *U.S. News and World Report*.

[2] *See, I Told You So*, New York: Pocket Books, 1993, p. 6.

[3] Commentary, *Los Angeles Times*, October 17, 1993.

[4] *Los Angeles Times*, October 20, 1993, p. B7.

[5] Editorial reply, KNX Radio, Los Angeles, August 4, 1988.

[6] *Los Angeles Times*, November 9, 1991, "Calendar" section, p. 1.

[7] *Los Angeles Times*, July 20, 1993, p. B8.

[8] "Destructive Themes in Rap Music Reveal a Lack of Hope," *National Minority Politics*, October 1993, p. 11.

[9] "My Rap Against Rap," *Reader's Digest*, May 1994, p. 63; condensed from *Washington Post*, November 14, 1993.

[10] *Los Angeles Times*, May 19, 1990, p. C3.

[11] Proverbs 13:12, Romans 8:25.